TOP 10 BUDAPEST

CRAIG TURP

EYEWITNESS TRAVEL

Left **Royal Palace from across the Danube** Right **Japanese Garden, Margaret Island**

LONDON, NEW YORK,
MELBOURNE, MUNICH AND DELHI
www.dk.com

Reproduced by Colourscan, Singapore Printed and bound in China by Leo Paper Group

First American Edition, 2006
10 11 12 13 10 9 8 7 6 5 4 3 2 1

Published in the United States by DK Publishing, Inc., 375 Hudson Street, New York, New York 10014

Reprinted with revisions 2008, 2010

Published in Great Britain by Dorling is Kindersley Limited.

A catalog record for this book is available from the Library of Congress.

ISSN 1479-344X
ISBN-978-0-75666-137-3

Within each Top 10 list in this book, no hierarchy of quality or popularity is implied. All 10 are, in the editor's opinion, of roughly equal merit.

Contents

Budapest's Top 10

The information in this DK Eyewitness Top 10 Travel Guide is checked regularly.
Every effort has been made to ensure that this book is as up-to-date as possible at the time of going to press. Some details, however, such as telephone numbers, opening hours, prices, gallery hanging arrangements and travel information are liable to change. The publishers cannot accept responsibility for any consequences arising from the use of this book, nor for any material on third party websites, and cannot guarantee that any website address in this book will be a suitable source of travel information. We value the views and suggestions of our readers very highly. Please write to: Publisher, DK Eyewitness Travel Guides, Dorling Kindersley, 80 Strand, London, WC2R 0RL, Great Britain.

Cover: Front - **DK Images:** Dorota Jarymowiczowie cbl; **Getty Images:** Jim Doberman main. Spine - **DK Images:** Dorota Jarymowiczowie b. Back - **Alamy Images:** Kevin Galvin cl; **DK Images:** Gabor Barka cr; Demetrio Carrasco c.

Left **Gobelin tapestry, Parliament** Centre **Gellért Baths** Right **Onyx Restaurant**

Around Town

Streetsmart

Left **Interior of Mátyás Church** Right **Liberty Bridge**

Key to abbreviations
Adm *admission charge* **Dis. access** *disabled access* **Ft** *forint*

BUDAPEST'S TOP 10

TOP 10 Budapest's Highlights

The finest of the Habsburg triumvirate of Budapest, Vienna and Prague, the Hungarian capital is much grander in scale than the Austrian and Czech capitals. Comprising three separate towns – hilly Buda and Óbuda on the Danube's western bank, and flat Pest on the eastern bank, this is a city rich in historical sights, including the Roman ruins of Aquincum, the Turkish baths and the Neo-Gothic Parliament. At night it buzzes with lively bars and clubs, and offers some top-quality options for eating out.

1 Hungarian Parliament

Viewed from the opposite bank of the Danube, the façade of the Hungarian Parliament is one of Budapest's defining sights. Its endless rooms contain boundless treasures *(see pp8–11)*.

2 St Stephen's Basilica

With its 96-m (315-ft) high dome visible from all over Budapest, St Stephen's Basilica houses the city's most bizarre relic – the mummified forearm of King István *(see pp12–13)*.

3 Váci utca

For centuries, Váci Street has been the centre of the Hungarian commercial world. Traders, swindlers, prostitutes and gentlemen all mingled in the street's packed hostelries and shops *(see pp14–15)*.

4 Gellért Hotel and Baths

Budapest is famous for its numerous thermal baths, and the best are the indoor and outdoor pools at the legendary Gellért Hotel *(see pp16–17)*.

5 Margaret Island

Isolated until the 19th century and long a retreat for religious contemplation, the lush and still secluded Margaret Island is an ideal place for a peaceful stroll *(see pp18–19)*.

Previous pages: **River Danube with Mátyás Church in the distance**

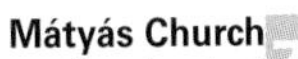

6 Hungarian National Gallery

The six permanent exhibitions spread throughout much of Budapest's Royal Palace present the most valuable collection of Hungarian art in the world *(see pp20–23)*.

7 Mátyás Church

The coronation church of the Hungarian kings, with its Gothic spire towering above much of Upper Buda, is as impressive close up as it is from afar *(see pp24–5)*.

8 State Opera House

Built to rival the opera houses of Vienna and Dresden, Budapest's sublime State Opera House is best viewed while taking in one of its world-class performances *(see pp26–7)*.

9 Hungarian National Museum

The Hungarian National Museum is a treasure trove of exhibits and artifacts from every period of Hungary's turbulent history *(see pp30–31)*.

10 Statue Park & Memento Park

Almost all of Hungary's Communist-era statues, which once stood in the public squares, are now displayed at this bizarre, but fascinating, open-air museum on the outskirts of Budapest *(see pp32–3)*.

Újlipótváros
Lipótváros
Terézváros
Belváros
V
Újpesti rakpart
Pannónia u
Szent István körút
Váci út
Nyugati tér
Honvéd u
Honvéd tér
Alkotmány u
Báthory u
Vértanúk tere
Szabadság tér
Bajcsy-Zsilinszky út
Podmaniczky u
Teréz körút
Nagymező u
Jókai tér
Liszt F. tér
Andrássy út
Október 6 u
Király u
Klauzál tér
József Attila u
Erzsébet tér
Bécsi u
Vörösmarty tér
Szervita tér
Váci u
Károly körút
Rákóczi út
Kossuth L. u
Múzeum körút
Belgrád rakpart
Szabad sajtó út
Petőfi S. u
Pollack M. tér
Elizabeth Bridge
Kálvin tér
Duna (Danube)
Üllői út
Szent Gellért rakpart
Vámház körút
Csarnok tér
Liberty Bridge
Közraktár u
Műegyetem rakpart
Bartók Béla út
10km
500 yards 0 metres 500

Top 10 Hungarian Parliament

In 1846, the Hungarian poet Mihály Vörösmarty wrote with some desperation that "the motherland has no home". When Hungary opened its magnificent Parliament building after decades of construction in 1902, it not only had a home, but one of the finest Neo-Gothic buildings in Europe. The largest Parliament building in the world at the time, it stood as a symbol of Hungarian self-confidence in the early 20th century. Designed by Imre Steindl, it is one of Budapest's defining landmarks, surpassed only by the Royal Palace.

One of a pair of lions at the main entrance

Ceiling of the dome with its Neo-Gothic gilding

The only way to see all the building's attractions is to join one of the guided tours that are available when Parliament is not in session.

Find out if Parliament is in session and book a ticket by calling 441 49 04 (English spoken).

There is no café on the premises, but the Ethnographical Museum just across the road has a café in its entrance hall.

- *Map J1*
- *V, Kossuth Lajos tér 1–3*
- *441 49 04*
- *Daily tours in English at 10am, noon, 1pm and 2pm. Ask at Gate 10, where the tour starts, about other language tours. Tours are free for EU citizens, but cost Ft2,820 for all others*
- *Dis. access*
- *www.parlament.hu*

Top 10 Attractions

1. Cross-Danube Vista
2. Grand Staircase
3. Main Entrance
4. Crown Jewels
5. Domed Hall
6. National Assembly Hall
7. Delegation Room
8. The Conquest
9. Congress Hall
10. Presidential Suite

1 Cross-Danube Vista

Sensational close up, Hungary's Parliament is arguably even better from afar. Set along the banks of the Danube *(right)*, its spires and symmetry can be admired from the other side of the river.

2 Grand Staircase

Sweeping upwards from the entrance, the sumptuous main staircase *(left)* has three outstanding ceiling frescoes. These include Károly Lotz's *Glorification of Hungary*, depicting allegorical moments in Hungary's history.

3 Main Entrance

Inspired by London's Houses of Parliament and built with no limitations on money, the main entrance is guarded by two huge lions sculpted by Béla Markup and József Somogyi.

4 Crown Jewels

Spirited out of Hungary after World War II, and stored in Fort Knox, USA till 1978, the Crown Jewels – the Crown of St Stephen *(left)* and the Royal Sceptre – are now kept in the Domed Hall.

5 Domed Hall

The spiritual heart of the building, the Domed Hall *(right)* was once used to host joint sessions of Parliament. The hall honours 16 Hungarian kings – each of the 16 pillars supporting the dome features a statue of a leader *(see pp10–11)*. Today, it is used for official ceremonies.

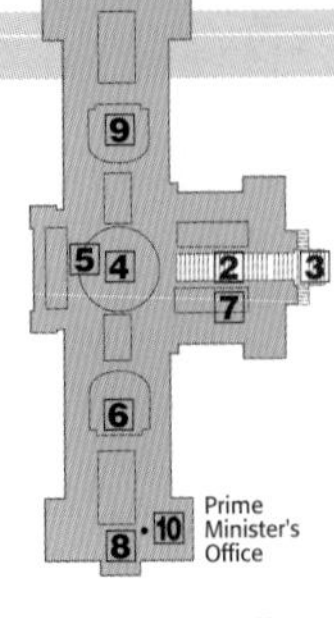

9 Congress Hall

Unused since 1944, when Hungary became a unicameral state, the former Hungarian Upper House *(below)* has a rich interior with a fine painting by Zsigmond Vajda of the monk Astrik handing St Stephen his crown.

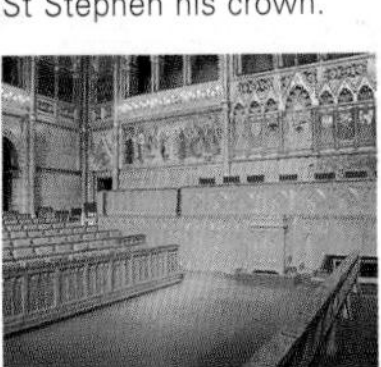

6 National Assembly Hall

The Hungarian Lower House *(right)* is where the Parliament sits – take a seat and dream of power. The bullet hole above the lectern dates from 1912, when an assassin attempted to kill the speaker, István Tisza.

7 Delegation Room

A relic of the Dual Monarchy *(see p70)*, this was where parliamentarians met delegates of the ministries. Its walls have artworks by Andor Dudits, while the ceiling paintings, *Wisdom* and *Fortitude*, are by Károly Lotz.

8 The Conquest

The building's finest work of art is Munkácsy's The *Conquest*. Originally intended for the Chamber of Commons, it was rejected as it was thought to misrepresent the first contact between the invading Magyars and Pannonian tribes – as a peaceful meeting rather than a heroic conquest.

10 Prime Minister's Office

Hungary's prime minister has an office here but it is closed to visitors. However, you can admire the reception rooms, which house 1930s paintings by Géza Udvary and Antal Diósy.

Imre Steindl

Before submitting his entry for the competition to design Hungary's Parliament, Imre Steindl also submitted designs for a proposed parliament in Berlin. His plans were rejected, and the winning entry, of course, was Paul Wallot's Reichstag. Berlin's loss was Hungary's gain as Steindl's vision resulted in a masterpiece. He is remembered by a bust, cast by Alajos Stróbl, on the main staircase.

The limestone used for surfacing the Parliament building began crumbling soon after it opened, and renovations continue to this day.

Left **Statue of Prince Árpád** Right **St Stephen (István), the Magyars' first Christian king**

Top 10 Domed Hall Statues

1 Árpád

Prince Árpád was chosen as the leader of the Magyar tribes shortly after they settled on the Pannonian plains in 896. The Magyars migrated from the Ural mountains in present-day Russia.

2 St Stephen

St Stephen (István) was elected Duke of the Magyars in AD 997. He adopted Christianity soon after, and was crowned king by Pope Sylvester II in 1001.

3 St Ladislaus

Hungary's ruler between 1077 and 1095, Ladislaus fought successful wars against the Turks and the Cumans and annexed Croatia in 1092.

King Mátyás Corvinus

4 András II

The son of King Béla III and brother of Emeric, András II was crowned in 1205. He greatly expanded the Magyar state eastwards, conquering large swathes of Transylvania and encouraging vast numbers of Magyars to settle in the region.

Main Staircase

5 Béla IV

Defeated by the Tatars in 1241, Béla IV survived to rebuild Hungary after the Tatars left the country in ashes a year later. His patient rebuilding of the nation over the next 25 years elevated him to greatness.

6 Louis I

Crowned in 1342, Louis the Great reigned for 40 years, expanding the Magyar kingdom with victories over Venice and Dalmatia between 1357 and 1358. In 1370, he formed a political union with Poland after the death of his uncle, the Polish king Casimir III, and ruled as sovereign of the two countries until his death in 1382.

7 János Hunyadi

János Hunyadi was born to a Romanian family of Vlach nobles who had long served the Hungarian king Sigismund. A gifted commander, János became the ruler of Transylvania in 1441, and then Governor of Hungary in 1446. He is best remembered for defeating the Turks in the Battle of Belgrade in 1456.

8 Mátyás Corvinus

The second son of János, Mátyás was born in Cluj-Napoca, Transylvania, and is generally considered to be the greatest of all Hungarian kings. Crowned in 1458 at the age of 15, he was a Renaissance man who valued the sciences, arts and architecture, inviting foreign writers, humanists, musicians and artists to his court. The first Hungarian printing press and library were founded during his 32-year reign.

9 Charles III

In 1687, Hungary finally succumbed to Austrian domination and renounced its right to elect its own king. Thereafter, the Habsburgs inherited the throne and Charles VI, the last Holy Roman Emperor of the direct Habsburg line, became Charles VI King of Bohemia as well as Charles III King of Hungary. The king spent much of his reign ensuring that his daughter, Maria Theresa, would succeed him.

10 Maria Theresa

Maria Theresa acceded to the throne in 1740, cementing Hungary's position as an integral part of the Habsburg Empire. Budapest became an imperial city and the magnificent Habsburg Royal Palace was built during her reign. The city also became a centre of Central European art, second only to Vienna. Maria ruled Hungary until her death in 1780.

Top 10 Dates in the Parliament's History

1. 1885 Foundation stone laid, 12 Oct
2. 1896 First session of Parliament, 15 Mar
3. 1902 Parliament building completed
4. 1912 Assassin attempts to shoot speaker, 4 Jun
5. 1920 Treaty of Trianon strips Hungary of two-thirds of its territory, 4 Jun
6. 1944 Hungary becomes a unicameral Republic
7. 1955 Parliament withdraws from the bloc of Soviet-backed nations
8. 1958 Execution of Prime Minister Imre Nagy, Jun
9. 1989 Communists allow multi-party elections, Oct
10. 1990 MPs take their seats after post-Communist elections, 2 May

The Domed Hall

The first section of the Parliament to be completed was the Domed Hall in 1896. It was used for a special session of Parliament held during Budapest's Millennium Celebrations. The 16-sided dome – which, at 96 m (315 ft), is the same height as that of St Stephen's Basilica – was designed to convey a sense of amplified space. Each of the 16 pillars supporting the dome bears the statue and coat of arms of a significant Hungarian ruler. Apart from the ten dignitaries mentioned above, the six remaining statues represent (in a clockwise direction) Könyves Kálmán, András III, István Báthory, István Bocskai, Gábor Bethlen and Leopold II.

Magnificent ceiling of the Domed Hall

St István's Coronation

TOP 10 St Stephen's Basilica

More than worthy of St Stephen (see p34), the Basilica that carries his name is visible from all over Budapest. Splendidly lit in the evening, it is perhaps the most photographed sight in the city. The dome, at 96 m (315 ft), is the exact height as that of the Parliament, whose builders decided not to go higher. It was built from 1851 to 1905 in the form of a Greek cross, and is the work of three successive architects – József Hild, Miklós Ybl and József Kauser.

Statue of St Matthew on the façade

Every year on St Stephen's Day (20 Aug), the Holy Right Hand is carried by the Basilica's priests past large crowds of people who gather in front of the Basilica. Arrive early to witness the spectacle.

A stone's throw away from the Basilica is Duran's, a sandwich shop ideal for lunch. It is located about 200 m (656 ft) south of the Basilica, at 7 Bajcsy-Zsilinszky út.

- *Map L2*
- *V, Szent István tér*
- *317 28 59*
- *Open church: 9am–5pm Mon–Fri, 9am–1pm Sat, 1–5pm Sun; treasury: 9am–5pm daily; tower: Apr–May & Sep–Oct 10am–4:30pm daily; Jun–Aug 9:30am–6pm daily*
- *Adm: Free (church); Ft400 (treasury); Ft500 dome viewing platform*
- *Dis. access*

Top 10 Features

1. Dome and Mosaics
2. North Tower
3. Main Altar
4. Main Entrance
5. Holy Right Hand
6. Main Portal
7. St Gellért and St Emeryka
8. Treasury
9. Gyula Benczúr Painting
10. Figures of the 12 Apostles

1 Dome and Mosaics

The Neo-Renaissance dome was designed by Miklós Ybl in 1867 after the original dome – designed by József Hild – caved in due to poor workmanship and materials. It is decorated with mosaics *(right)* by Károly Lotz. A viewing platform above the cupola is reached by a lift and stairs.

2 North Tower

The 9,144-kg (9-ton) bell in the North Tower was paid for by German Catholics, who were ashamed that the Nazis had looted the original during their retreat from Budapest at the end of World War II. The original bell was never traced.

3 Main Altar

A life-size marble statue of St Stephen (King István), by sculptor Alajos Stróbl, dominates the main altar *(left)* of the Basilica. On either side, fine paintings by the 19th-century artist Gyula Benczúr depict scenes from the saint-king's life.

4 Main Entrance

"I am the way and the truth and the life" proclaims the Latin inscription above the Basilica's main entrance. Situated above the inscription are several statues of Hungarian saints paying homage to the Virgin Mary and the infant Jesus.

5 Holy Right Hand

The mummified forearm of St Stephen *(right)* is displayed in the Holy Right Hand Chapel near the main altar. It was taken to Dubrovnik in Croatia by Béla IV in the 13th century to protect it from the Tatars. After stints in Vienna and at the Royal Palace in Buda, it was brought here on 20 August 1945 – St Stephen's Day.

6 Main Portal

The colossal main door *(above)* features carvings depicting the heads of the 12 Apostles. Impressive from afar, it is beginning to look a little worse for wear when seen close up.

7 St Gellért and St Emeryka

Alajos Stróbl carved the statue of Bishop St Gellért and his pupil, St Emeryka (St Stephen's son Imre), that stands in a small nave in the centre of the main hall. Opposite is another statue – St Elizabeth by Károly Senyei.

8 Treasury

A replica of the holy Hungarian crown is the centerpiece of a small but splendid collection of religious jewellery. The original crown is now kept in the Hungarian Parliament *(see pp8–11)*. Gifts to Hungarian kings from a succession of popes are also on display.

9 Gyula Benczúr Painting

St Stephen, by Gyula Benczúr *(below)*, is one of the most important works in the Hungarian artistic cannon. It portrays the king – who died without an heir – proffering the care of the country and the crown to the Virgin Mary.

10 Figures of the 12 Apostles

The Basilica's rear colonnade has 12 superb statues by Leó Feszler representing the 12 Apostles. Below is a fine Neo-Classical loggia.

Organ Concerts

The Basilica's organ was made by Angster & Sons of Pécs, and installed in 1904. At the time, it was considered the world's finest. The organ was enlarged in 1934, and today comprises no less than 5,898 pipes. You can hear it at special organ concerts, which are held in the Basilica from time to time.

The Basilica was seriously damaged during World War II, and major renovation between 1983 and 1989 restored it to its former glory.

TOP 10 Váci utca

Váci utca is quite simply the heart and soul of Budapest. A street in two parts – the southern end for shopping and the northern end for drinking and eating – it buzzes with life day and night, and acts as the city's commercial and social hub. Although it is cut in half by the access road to Elizabeth Bridge, only a part of the street's southern end is open to traffic. To get a real feel for Budapest, you should stroll down its full length.

1 Vörösmarty tér Metro Station

The tiled walls, wooden booths and platforms of this immaculate 1903 station *(above)* are a reminder of why underground railways were considered glamorous. The Lilliputian yellow trains are enchanting too.

Metro station sign

As with any place that attracts crowds, beware of pickpockets operating the length of Váci utca, as well as attractive blondes who invite men for a drink in the evenings *(see p106)*.

Although Gerbeaud Cukrászda is the more famous coffee house, the Taverna Hotel's own coffee shop is another great place to unwind.

- *Map C5*
- *Gerbeaud Cukrászda: V, Vörösmarty tér 7; 429 90 00; Open 9am–9pm daily; www.gerbeaud.hu*
- *Cucina: Taverna Hotel, Váci utca 20; 266 41 44*
- *Fontana Department Store: Váci utca 16; 266 64 00*
- *Thonet House: Váci utca 11*
- *Herendi Márkabolt: Váci utca 19–21; 266 63 05; Open 10am–7pm daily*
- *1000 Tea: Váci utca 65; 337 82 17*

Top 10 Attractions

1. Vörösmarty Tér Metro Station
2. The Promenade
3. Gerbeaud Cukrászda
4. Fontana Department Store
5. Klotild Palaces
6. Thonet House
7. Herendi Márkabolt
8. St Michael's City Church
9. Central Market Hall
10. 1000 Tea

2 The Promenade

Walk the full length of Váci utca *(right)* from Vörösmarty tér to Vámház körút and take in the atmosphere, the bustle and the stunning architecture of the street's buildings. You won't be alone during the summer, but the crowds are a part of the appeal.

3 Gerbeaud Cukrászda

This is the most famous coffee house in Budapest. Since 1858, Gerbeaud Cukrászda *(left)* has been renowned for its richly decorated interior and immaculate service.

4 Fontana Department Store

The Modernist Fontana Store *(right)* complements Váci utca's older buildings. Built in the 1980s, it marked the beginning of a new consumerist trend and now houses outlets such as C&A, as well as fashion labels, sports gear, cosmetics and a café.

5 Klotild Palaces

Forming a splendid entrance to Elizabeth Bridge, the twin Klotild Palaces *(right)* were commissioned by Archduchess Klotild, daughter-in-law of Emperor Franz József, and completed in 1902. Much of the buildings' interiors are now occupied by shops or used as office space.

7 Herendi Márkabolt

Herendi ceramics are famous for their intricacy and quality, and this outlet is one of the few places you can be sure of finding the genuine article.

9 Central Market Hall

Budapest's largest market *(above)* has innumerable stalls on the ground floor selling fruit, vegetables, fish and cheese. Specialities are spicy *kolbász* salami and sheep's cheese. The upper-level stalls sell local crafts *(see p50)*.

10 1000 Tea

Váci utca has lots of places to eat, drink and while away the hours, but a relaxing oasis away from the hustle and bustle is 1000 Tea. This quiet café has a selection of loose-leaf teas from all over the world as well as music to soothe the spirit. It is a great place to rest after a day out shopping.

8 St Michael's City Church

First built around 1230, St Michael's City Church (below) was devastated by the Turks in 1541, rebuilt in 1701 and then renovated between 1964 and 1968. Its plain exterior belies a rich interior, including a fine gold pulpit and impressive dome.

6 Thonet House

Built from 1888 to 1890 by Ödön Lechner and Gyula Pártos, Thonet House once belonged to a wealthy family. Zsolnay ceramics *(above)* adorn the walls, while the shop sells exclusive crystal.

Váci utca

The name of Budapest's most famous street originated rather simply. The street was once the main road connecting Pest to the town of Vác *(see p59)*, 40 km (25 miles) north of Budapest. The gate leading to Vác used to stand at Váci utca No. 3.

Stained-glass window by Bózó Stanisits

TOP 10 Gellért Hotel and Baths

The Gellért Hotel is the finest of all the great bath houses in Budapest. Its main swimming pool is perhaps the best example of Neo-Classical architecture in Hungary, and is certainly the ideal place to enjoy Budapest's warm therapeutic waters. The hotel itself is a fine Secessionist piece, designed by Ármin Hegedűs, Artúr Sebestyén and Izidor Sterk, and built between 1912 and 1918. It was damaged by heavy bombing in World War II and rebuilt in the late 1940s.

Outdoor wave pool

Swimming costumes and towels can be hired at the baths, but are expensive and not very good, so it's best to bring your own.

The pricing structure at the Gellért, and all baths for that matter, is Byzantine to say the least. Standard entry includes access to the baths and swimming pool, but nothing else. You will, however, receive a refund if you stay less than two hours. Children of all ages pay almost full price.

- *Map L6*
- *Gellért Hotel: XI, Szent Gellért tér 1; 889 55 00; www.danubiushotels.com/gellert*
- *Gellért Baths: XI, Kelenhegyi út 4; 466 61 66; open summer: 6am–7pm daily; winter: 6am–7pm Mon–Fri, 6am– 5pm Sat & Sun; adm Ft3,600 (baths & pool); Dis. access www.budapestspas.hu*
- *Terrace Restaurant & Café Eszpresszó: a three-course meal for one costs Ft7,500–10,000*

Top 10 Features

1. Façade
2. Main Entrance Hall
3. Main Staircase
4. Terrace
5. Café Eszpresszó
6. Bath Foyers
7. Main Swimming Pool
8. Outdoor Pools
9. Thermal Baths
10. Eastern-Style Towers

1 Façade

The Gellért's Secession-era façade *(below)* reflects the self-confidence that befits a building constructed during the final phase of the Habsburg Empire, when Hungary was on the verge of independence.

2 Main Entrance Hall

With its elaborate mosaics, plush carpets and over-the-top statues, the hotel's entrance hall is a leap into the past. The staff are patient and helpful with visitors who just want to admire the scene.

3 Main Staircase

The stained-glass windows *(below)* on the staircase landings were designed by Bózó Stanisits. They illustrate a legend about a magic stag, recorded in János Arany's poetry.

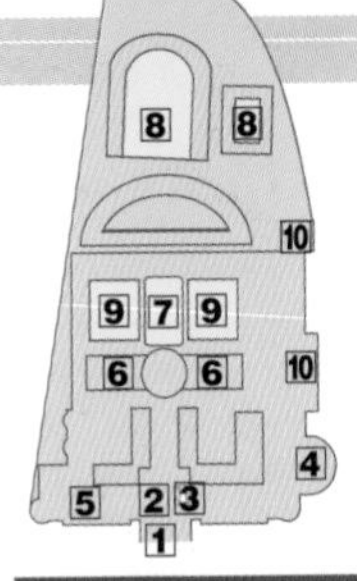

4 Terrace

There's no better place to enjoy a hearty and relaxed Sunday brunch in Budapest than on the well-shaded, first-floor terrace of the Gellért Hotel. The panoramic views from here over the Danube and the city are simply magnificent.

5 Café Eszpresszó

An old-fashioned coffee and teahouse with a range of cakes and pastries *(below)*. You are served by liveried waitresses, and the Viennese-style furniture adds to the splendour of the place.

6 Bath Foyers

There are three foyers at the entrance. The central foyer's glass roof is the highlight, but the floors, walls, statuettes and benches of the others are all marvellous as well. A small fee entitles you to walk around without actually entering the baths.

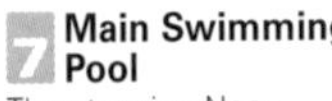

7 Main Swimming Pool

The stunning Neo-Classical main pool *(left)* is the finest part of the Gellért baths. Surrounded by high galleries and marble columns, it is decorated with colourful mosaics. Don't miss taking a dip, as swimming here is indeed a luxurious experience.

8 Outdoor Pools

During the summer, bathers head to the hotel's outdoor pools *(above)* and sun terraces. The main outdoor pool was one of the first in the world to have an artificial wave mechanism, which is still in use today.

9 Thermal Baths

The medicinal waters at this site were first discovered in the 13th century during the reign of King András II. During the Middle Ages, a hospital was built at this spot. Today, there is a great network of thermal baths at various temperatures. Currently undergoing renovation work, one bath will always be kept open.

10 Eastern-Style Towers

Although the Gellért is primarily a Secessionist building, its cylindrical, Eastern-style towers *(above)* commemorate the earlier Turkish baths which stood on this site.

Healing Waters

Although Budapest is known for its baths, few visitors realize the major role they play in city life, and how much faith the locals place in the healing properties of their waters. For many of the city's older residents, the baths remain as important as they were under the Ottomans, who developed the potential of Budapest's astonishing 120-odd thermal springs. Most of the city's thermal waters are highly sulphurous, and are said to be especially effective in treating rheumatism, arthritis and even Parkinson's disease.

Top 10 Margaret Island

Inhabited since Roman times, Margaret Island (Margitsziget) is a tranquil, green oasis in the middle of the Danube. It is named after Princess Margit (Margaret), daughter of King Béla IV, who spent most of her life in the island's former convent in the 13th century. It was a popular hunting ground for medieval kings, and monks were also drawn to its peace and quiet. The island has served as Budapest's playground since 1869 and is still the perfect escape from the city.

Relaxing in a park on Margaret Island

The easiest way to get to Margaret Island is by bus No. 26 from Nyugati Station. However, the most enjoyable way is by boat. There are irregular ferries from Vigadó tér to Esztergom and Visegrád throughout the summer, which stop at Margaret Island. Check the timetable at Vigadó tér for more details.

For lunch on the island, head to Palatinus Strand for doughnuts and hot dogs. For a more formal meal, visit the Danubius Grand Hotel Margitsziget.

- *Map B1*
- *Margaret Island (Margitsziget): Budapest XIII*

Top 10 Attractions

1. Dominican Church
2. Japanese Garden
3. Centenary Monument
4. Franciscan Church
5. Palatinus Strand
6. Water Tower
7. St Michael's Church
8. Bodor Well
9. Danubius Grand Hotel Margitsziget
10. Horse-Drawn Carriage Rides

2 Japanese Garden

The most delightful of the island's landscaped gardens is the Japanese garden *(right)* at the northern end. It has a wide variety of flowers as well as rock gardens and waterfalls.

3 Centenary Monument

The Modernist Centenary Monument *(above)* was raised in 1973 to commemorate the unification of Buda, Óbuda and Pest to form Budapest in 1873.

1 Dominican Church

One of the island's most important monuments is the ruin of a 13th-century Dominican convent. It was founded by Béla IV, whose daughter Margit came to live here in 1251. A plaque in the church marks the spot where she is buried.

4 Franciscan Church

The ruins of the 14th-century Franciscan church *(below)* lie secluded in the island's centre. Though there is little left to admire, it still has a fine arched window and a staircase.

Traffic is not allowed beyond the Danubius Grand Hotel and Thermal Hotel Margitsziget, so hire a four-seater bicycle from a rental kiosk.

5 Palatinus Strand

Opened in 1919, the city's largest outdoor pool complex *(right)* buzzes from dawn to dusk, as people enjoy the therapeutic waters pumped from the island's thermal springs *(see p37)*.

6 Water Tower

The UNESCO-protected Water Tower *(below)* was built in 1911 to supply fresh water to the Danubius GrandHotel Margitsziget. It stands 57 m (187 ft) high and a gallery offers panoramic views of the entire island.

7 St Michael's Church

The oldest building on the island, St Michael's Church *(below)* was founded in the 11th century, but was devastated by the Turks in 1541. What you see today is a 1930s reconstruction, using materials from the original building.

8 Bodor Well

The unusual musical Bodor Well *(left)* is, in fact, a copy of a long destroyed well, built in 1820 in Târgu Mures, Romania. This copy dates from 1936, and plays recorded music on the hour.

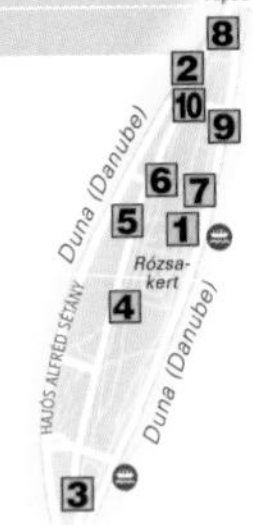

9 Danubius Grand Hotel Margitsziget

This legendary hotel designed by Miklós Ybl opened in 1872. For years, it was the most fashionable in the city, attracting aristocracy from all over Europe. Today, it has been joined by a sister spa *(see p113)*.

10 Horse-Drawn Carriage Rides

You can see the island in imperial style by taking a carriage ride *(above)*. Lasting about an hour, the rides start from the northern end of the island, opposite the hotels.

Princess Margit (Margaret)

After the horrors of the Mongol invasion and subsequent destruction of Budapest from 1241 to 1242, a desperate King Béla IV offered to give his daughter to God, if in return, He would ensure that the Mongols never returned. In 1251, Béla sent his nine-year-old daughter Margit to the island's convent, where she stayed for the rest of her life. The Mongols never returned.

The island is very popular with joggers and is a great place to come for a run. There are several cafés selling drinks and snacks en route.

TOP 10 Hungarian National Gallery

Nowhere in Budapest is there more treasure than at the Hungarian National Gallery, housed in a building which is itself very much part of the city's heritage. Established in 1975, when a large section of the Royal Palace was given over to it, the Gallery displays art from medieval times to the present day and comprises six permanent exhibitions which present the cream of Hungarian creative arts. The museum is especially strong in its portrayal of the Secession, the 19th-century movement that pushed boundaries and fused genres (see p23).

National Gallery façade

To see the very best of the museum, join a guided tour that includes the basement level Habsburg Crypt. Tours are in several languages, though you may have to wait for a large enough number of people to assemble before one begins.

The Gallery can be very crowded in the morning and early afternoon. Plan your visit for after 3pm.

Having admired the Gallery's many glories, take a walk into the Castle District for a refreshment at one of the numerous restaurants and cafés.

- *Map H4*
- *Buda Castle, Royal Palace, A, B, C, D wings*
- *356 00 49*
- *Open 10am–6pm Tue–Sun*
- *Adm Ft800*
- *Dis. access A wing*
- *www.mng.hu*

Top 10 Attractions

1. Main Entrance
2. The Visitation
3. Recapture of Buda Castle
4. Picnic in May
5. Women of Eger
6. Great Throne Room
7. Habsburg Crypt
8. The Yawning Apprentice
9. Birdsong
10. Woman Bathing

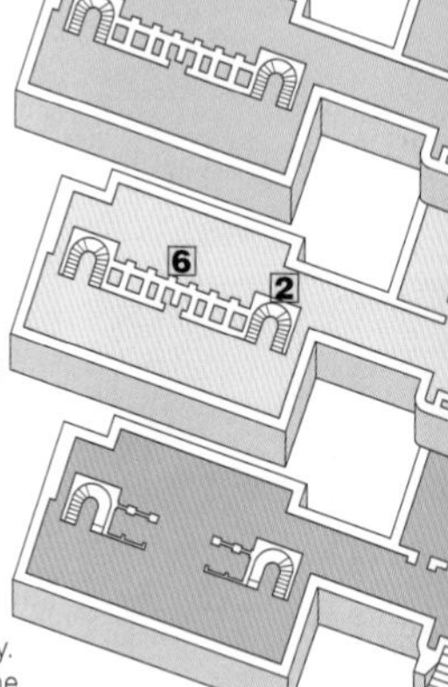

Key

- Ground Floor
- 1st Floor
- 2nd Floor
- 3rd Floor

1 Main Entrance

A part of the 18th-century Maria Theresa Palace, the museum's Neo-Classical façade has Germanic influences.

2 The Visitation

Nothing is known about the life of Master MS, the most important representative of late Gothic painting in Hungary. This painting *(below)* is the best of his works, depicting the meeting of the Virgin Mary and St Elizabeth.

3 Recapture of Buda Castle

Gyula Benczúr painted this for the 1896 Millennium Celebrations. It was intended to emphasize the necessity of Austro-Hungarian rule by showing that Hungary was only freed from Turkish suzerainty due to Karl of Lotharingia and Eugene of Savoy.

Many of the works on display were exhibited at the National Museum and the Museum of Fine Arts before the Gallery opened in 1957.

4 Picnic in May

Painted from memory in 1873 by Pál Szinyei-Merse, *Picnic in May (right)* evokes the French Impressionists. The figure lying with his back towards us is the artist himself.

5 Women of Eger

Besides his fine portrait work, Bertalan Székely painted a number of historical works featuring simple, heroic female figures in a romantic style. *Women of Eger* (1867), portrays the women of the town defending Eger Castle against the Turks.

6 Great Throne Room

An entire room of the Gallery is devoted to 15th- and 16th-century Gothic altarpieces. The best are the ones of St Anne and St John the Baptist (1520) from a church in Kisszeben (Sabinov, in present-day Slovakia).

7 Habsburg Crypt

This Crypt, with the exquisite sarcophagus of Palatine Archduke Joseph, is a Neo-Classical warren of black and white marble and gold leaf. It can only be seen on a guided tour.

8 The Yawning Apprentice

The Yawning Apprentice (1867) was the first renowned work by Mihály Munkácsy, Hungary's finest Realist. It is matchless in its extraordinary detail.

9 Birdsong

Károly Ferenczy was one of Hungary's finest artists of the late 19th–early 20th centuries. The soft *Birdsong (above)*, painted in 1893 while he was in Munich, is one of his best. The latter part of his life was spent depicting homo-erotic images of young men and boys.

10 Woman Bathing

Nudes were a speciality of Károly Lotz, who painted this particularly sensuous figure *(right)* in 1901. A fine example of Neo-Classical painting, it evokes the style of the French artist, Ingres. Lotz is also known for the murals in the Hungarian Parliament *(see pp8–11)*.

Mihály Munkácsy

Regarded as Hungary's finest artist, Mihály Munkácsy began his career making finished woodwork. After completing his first major painting in 1867, when he was just 23, he moved to Paris, where he painted a series of masterpieces including *The Churning Woman* and *Woman Carrying Brushwood*, both now in the National Gallery. He died in 1900 at the age of 55 in Paris.

Munkácsy also painted two monumental works – The Conquest *(see p9) and a fresco,* Apotheosis of Renaissance, *for a museum in Vienna.*

Left **Detail of János Vaszary's *The Golden Age*** Right **Hungarian National Gallery façade**

TOP 10 Secession Works in the Gallery

1 Lady in Red

József Rippl-Rónai (1861–1927) was one of the three most important artists of the Secession Movement. He studied for several years in Paris, at a time when the Art Nouveau movement was thriving. His masterpiece *Lady in Red* (1896), also known as *The Woman in Polka Dots*, depicts the somewhat affected pose of a model who was apparently caught by surprise. It was the first Secession-style painting in Hungary.

2 Girl with a Birdcage

An early painting by Rippl-Rónai, *Girl with a Birdcage* (1892) is renowned for its marvellous use of contrast – note the white of the girl's hands compared to the blurred, dark background. The slightly contrived pose of the model holding the cage is a trademark of the artist.

Girl with a Birdcage **by Rippl-Rónai**

3 The Manor House at Körtyvélyes

Rippl-Rónai visited Italy in 1904 and was fascinated by the decorative mosaics he saw in many homes. This work from 1907 anticipates his shift from soft brushwork to more forthright strokes, which would culminate in the bold paintings of his later years.

4 Girls Getting Dressed

Completed in 1912, this is a late Rippl-Rónai work that shows the progression of Secessionist painting as the brushstrokes became bolder and the colours brighter. The somewhat awkward pose of the girl on the left betrays the artist's penchant for playing with the viewer's perception.

5 The Golden Age

The second of the great Secessionist triumvirate, János Vaszary (1867–1939) oscillated between Art Nouveau and Post-Impressionism. His best painting is probably this 1898 Art Nouveau rendition of a nostalgic yearning for a lost paradise.

6 Fancy Dress Ball

Vaszary's brightly coloured 1907 portrayal of Budapest society has a touch of decadence. Notice the gentleman's leering expression and the licentious pose of the object of his affection.

7 **Breakfast in the Open Air**
This painting by Vaszary makes fabulous use of light and colour. At first glance, it seems to be a sympathetic depiction of Budapest society. Yet the indifference of the girl's parents towards her behaviour could be interpreted as a criticism of societal values at the time.

8 **Riders in the Park**
Dating from 1919, this is another fine example of late Secessionist painting by Vaszary, with sharp brush strokes and high contrast colours. The influence of Matisse, whom he knew from his sojourns in Paris, is clearly visible in this work.

9 **Magic**
Lajos Gulácsy (1882–1932), the youngest of the famous Secessionist trio, was a self-taught exponent of quasi-Surrealist art. His work Magic (1906) depicts an insecure male being reassured by a strong woman. Gulácsy himself was hopelessly insecure, and spent much of his later life in various psychiatric institutions.

10 **Self Portrait with Hat**
Lajos Gulácsy's *Self Portrait with Hat* (1912) reinforces his rather detached view of the world and perhaps his lack of belief in his own abilities. In the painting, his face wears an anxious and vulnerable expression.

Top 10 Secessionist Buildings

1. Gresham Palace Four Seasons Hotel *(Map K3)*
2. Gellért Hotel *(Map L6)*
3. Museum of Applied Arts *(Map D5)*
4. Geology Institute *(Map P2)*
5. Hungarian National Bank *(Map K2)*
6. Post Office Savings Bank *(Map L2)*
7. Városliget Calvinist Church *(Map E3)*
8. Franz Liszt Academy of Music *(Map D3)*
9. New York Palace *(Map E4)*
10. New Theatre *(Map M2)*

The Secession

From its quiet beginnings among avant-garde artists in Vienna in the late 1880s, until it gave way to Art Deco in the 1920s, the Secession Movement was a coherent attempt to break away from the romantic historicism of 19th-century art. It tried to find new forms of inspiration from the distant past, especially in the bold colours of Transylvanian folk art. Often characterized by fantastical designs, bright colours and stylized forms, the movement repossessed art from the clutches of nationalists, restoring the notion of art for art's sake. The movement encompassed all forms of the decorative and visual arts, from painting to sculpture and ceramics to interior design. It is perhaps best seen in the paintings that adorn the walls of the Hungarian National Gallery, the beautiful Zsolnay ceramics seen all over the city and, above all, in the architecture of the day.

Left **Zsolnay tiles on the roof of the Geology Institute** Right **Museum of Applied Arts**

Top 10 Mátyás Church

Rose window

The profusion of architectural styles in Mátyás Church betrays both the building's and the city's troubled history. After the original church was destroyed in 1241, a new church, part of Béla IV's fortified city, was built from 1255 to 1269. Much of this Gothic building remains, though it was Mátyás Corvinus, after whom the church is named, who expanded it in the 15th century. The final phase of restoration took place from 1873 to 1896, when Frigyes Schulek redesigned it in the Neo-Baroque style.

Béla Tower, Mátyás Church

A programme giving times and dates of all upcoming classical concerts, held two or three evenings a week during the summer, is available at the main entrance to the church.

Just across the square in front of the church and a short walk along Szentháromság utca, is Ruszwurm, one of Budapest's most historic cafés *(see p66)*.

- *Map H2*
- *I, Szentháromság tér 2*
- *355 56 57*
- *Open 9am–5pm Mon–Sat, 1–5pm Sun (may close Sat pm in summer for weddings)*
- *Adm Ft700*
- *Dis. access*
- *www.matyas-templom.hu*

Top 10 Features

1. Béla Tower
2. Hidden Images of King Louis
3. Mary Portal
4. Stained-Glass Windows
5. Loreto Chapel and Baroque Madonna
6. Sunday Mass
7. Tomb of King Béla III and Anne de Châtillon
8. Altar
9. Rose Window
10. Roof

1 Béla Tower

Named after Béla IV, the stout Béla Tower retains a number of its original Gothic features, though the spire and turrets are reconstructions. Note how the tower is the least embellished part of the church.

2 Hidden Images of King Louis

While entering the church through the main portal, turn around and look up to see images of King Louis the Great and his wife on the uppermost pillar beside the portal *(above)*. These sculptures date from the 14th century.

Central nave, Mátyás Church

3 Mary Portal

The Assumption of the Blessed Virgin Mary is the finest example of Gothic stone carving in Hungary. Frigyes Schulek reconstructed the portal *(left)* in the 19th century, using surviving fragments of the original building.

St Stephen first raised a church here around 1015, though that early church, known as St Mary's, was destroyed by the Tatars in 1241.

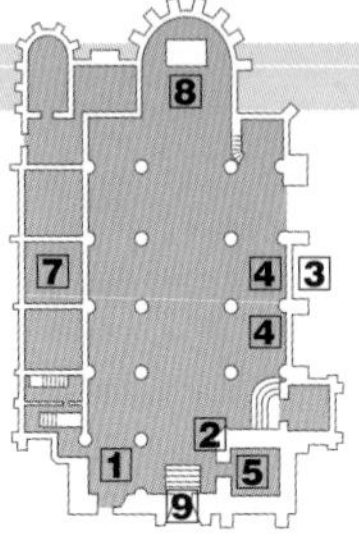

4 Stained-Glass Windows
Designed by Frigyes Schulek and painted by Károly Lotz, the three windows on the church's southern side depict the Virgin Mary's life, the family of Béla IV and the life of St Elizabeth of Árpádház, who married at 13, divorced at 19 and died at 24.

6 Sunday Mass
The church's two 1909 Rieger organs, restored in 1984, are the finest in Hungary. Sunday Mass, held at 10am, features the organs and the church's choir. A traditional centre of spiritual music, the church also plays host to more than 100 concerts a year.

7 Tomb of King Béla III and Anne de Châtillon
Frigyes Schulek designed this elaborate tomb *(above)* after the mortal remains of Béla III and his first wife had been found during excavations at Székesfehérvár Cathedral in 1862.

9 Rose Window
The Neo-Gothic Rose Window above the Main Portal was recreated by Frigyes Schulek after he unearthed fragments of the original during the restoration of the church. The original had been bricked up during the Baroque period.

10 Roof
The splendid multi-coloured tiled roof *(above)* is a recent addition, built between 1950 and 1970. The original roof, a plain affair, burnt down after Soviet shelling during the siege of Buda in 1944–5.

5 Loreto Chapel and Baroque Madonna
Legend has it that in 1686, the Madonna *(right)* appeared before the Turks defending Buda Castle, who saw it as a sign of imminent defeat. Habsburg troops took the castle that very night.

8 Altar
The early Gothic-style altar *(above)* features a replica of the holy Hungarian crown atop a statue of the Virgin Mary. A shrine to the Madonna, it was designed by Frigyes Schulek and completed in 1893.

King Mátyás
One of the greatest figures in Hungarian history, King Mátyás is often claimed by both Romanians and Serbs as being one of their own. What's certain is that Matei Corvin, as he is known in Romania, was born in Cluj-Napoca, in present-day Romania. He was the son of János Hunyadi, who in turn was the grandson of native Serbs. His family origins remain one of the main causes of tension between Hungarian and Romanian historians *(see p11)*.

Much of the church's original details were lost when it was turned into the Great Mosque by the Turks in 1541.

TOP 10 State Opera House

Nowhere in Budapest is the ancien regime as alive and well as at the State Opera House, architect Miklós Ybl's magnum opus. A Neo-Renaissance masterpiece built in 1884, when money was simply not an issue, its interior is a study in opulence and grandeur. A rival to any opera house in the world, its roll-call of musical directors reads like a who's who of Central European music – Ferenc Erkel, Gustav Mahler, Otto Klemperer, among others.

Lamp with putti

Main stage, Opera House

Admire the façade, the main entrance and the foyer throughout the day, as the ticket office is open daily from 11am to 5pm. To see the rest of the building, you will either need to attend an opera or join a guided tour, available in English, Hungarian, German, Spanish, Serbo-Croat, Dutch and Italian.

Concert tickets are usually cheap, as subsidies keep prices low *(see p109).*

Opposite the Opera House, at 8 Dalszínház utca, is the good-value Belcanto Italian restaurant *(see p79)*, famous for it waiters, who occasionally break into song.

- *Map M2*
- *VI, Andrássy út 22*
- *State Opera House: 332 79 14; Box office: 353 01 70*
- *Guided tours at 3pm and 4pm daily, Ft2,800*
- *Dis. access*
- *www.opera.hu*

Top 10 Features

1. Façade
2. Main Entrance
3. Statues of Liszt and Erkel
4. Foyer
5. Foyer Murals
6. Main Staircase
7. Chandelier
8. Main Stage
9. Royal Box
10. Museum

1 Façade

The passage of time has been kind to Andrássy út, and the State Opera House is not as hemmed in as many of the city's other significant buildings. While in no way unique, the façade *(above)*, made of colonnades, balconies and loggias, is impressive.

2 Main Entrance

Stand under the State Opera House's sublime entrance with its muraled ceilings, and you will immediately wish you were part of 19th-century Budapest society, stepping out of a horse-drawn carriage to attend a premiere.

3 Statues of Liszt and Erkel

The busts of Hungary's two greatest composers – Liszt *(left)* and Erkel – stand guard on either side of the entrance. Both were sculpted by Alajos Stróbl, who was responsible for much of the building's interior design.

4 Foyer

The foyer is a wonderful riot of murals, columns, chandeliers and gilded vaulted ceilings. Ostentation to rival Vienna was the order of the day, and Ybl did not disappoint his patrons.

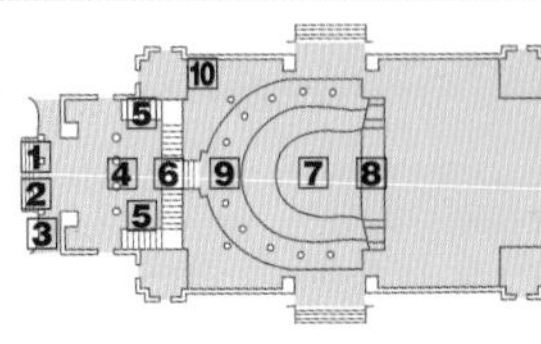

5 Foyer Murals

Painted by Bertalan Székely and Mór Than, the foyer's sensational murals *(above)* cover the entire ceiling and depict the nine Muses and other allegorical scenes.

6 Main Staircase

A red carpet covers the marble stairs *(below)* beneath a huge chandelier in another of the State Opera House's classic set pieces. The gilded panels of the ceiling contain nine paintings by Than, showing the awakening and triumph of music.

7 Chandelier

Above the auditorium, a 2,722-kg (3-ton) Mainz chandelier *(above)* illuminates a magnificent fresco by Károly Lotz of the Greek gods on Olympus. The chimney above it facilitates ventilation.

8 Main Stage

During the building of the Opera, the Vienna Ring Theatre was destroyed by fire. As a safety measure, an iron safety curtain, all-metal stage hydraulics and a sprinkler system were installed, making the Hungarian Opera the most modern theatre in the world.

9 Royal Box

Ybl always insisted that the Royal Box was his finest achievement. Decorated with sculptures symbolizing the four operatic voices – soprano, alto, tenor and bass – it is in the centre of a circle of three-tiered boxes.

10 Museum

The museum *(above)* houses memorabilia of famous performers who have graced this stage. Sándor Svéd, a renowned Hungarian baritone, who performed at New York's Metropolitan for years, features prominently.

Bánk Bán

Hungary's most famous opera, *Bánk Bán*, was written by Ferenc Erkel and premiered in 1861. The story begins with Otto, brother of András II, who plans to seduce the wife of a faithful Hungarian viceroy, Bánk Bán. The knight Biberach tells Bán of Otto's dastardly scheme, and Bán decides to join a rebellion against the court. Rarely performed today, it was turned into a film by Csaba Kael in 2001.

Check The Budapest Times (see p105) *for opera schedules.*

Hungarian National Museum

Since its founding in 1802, Budapest's most fascinating museum has been home to Hungary's finest collection of art, artifacts, photographs and documents relating to the country's troubled history. The building that houses the collection is a timeless piece of Neo-Classical architecture designed by Mihály Pollack, while the impressive interior has frescoes by Károly Lotz and Mór Than.

Façade, National Museum

The Hungarian National Museum is set on three levels. The basement displays Roman mosaics, the first floor is home to exhibits from the 5th century BC to the Middle Ages, and the second floor houses exhibits from the 12th century to the present day.

The famous Múzeum Kávéház és Étterem (see p87), located next to the National Museum, is the perfect place to relax with a cup of coffee after viewing the museum's collection.

- *Map M5*
- *VIII, Múzeum körút 14–16*
- *338 21 22*
- *Open 10am–6pm Tue–Sun*
- *Adm Ft1,000*
- *Dis. access*
- *www.mnm.hu*

Top 10 Features

1. Museum Steps
2. Coronation Mantle
3. Diadem
4. Golden Stag
5. Funeral Crown
6. Byzantine Crown
7. Mozart's Clavichord
8. Processional Crucifix
9. Throne Carpet
10. Campaigning in Front of the National Museum

1 Museum Steps

History was made here *(above)* in 1848, when Sándor Petőfi recited his poem *Nemzeti Dal* (National Song) and the 12 *pont* (12 points), which led to an uprising against the Habsburgs. The event is commemorated each year.

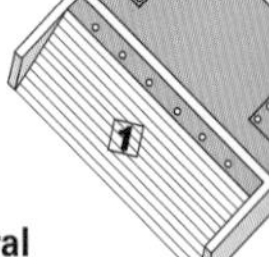

2 Coronation Mantle

This silk gown with the figures of Christ and the Apostles *(below)* was given to a church in Székesfehérvár by St Stephen in 1031. It later became a coronation coat for the Árpád kings.

3 Diadem

Dating from the Hun period in the 5th century AD, the stunning gold diadem is the most ancient of its kind. It was found in Csorna and is studded with 158 precious stones.

4 Golden Stag

A hand-forged figure from the 6th century BC, the Golden Stag was part of a Scythian prince's shield. It is in almost flawless condition.

5 Funeral Crown

Found in Margaret Island's Dominican church in 1838, this golden crown *(below)* dates from the 13th century and was worn by a female member of an Árpád family on her deathbed.

6 Byzantine Crown

The exquisitely crafted Byzantine crown is of particular value, as it is made of gold leaf that dates back to between 1042 and 1050. The gold leaf is decorated with allegories of the Great Virtues, which were popular in Byzantine art.

7 Mozart's Clavichord

This travelling clavichord was bought for the young Wolfgang Amadeus Mozart by his father, Leopold Mozart. It was used by the child prodigy to practice upon during their concert tours.

Key

	1st Floor
	2nd Floor

8 Processional Crucifix

The use of crucifixes on altars became widepread in the Western Church in the 12th century. This crucifix *(left)* from Szerecseny dates from that period. A similar piece lies in the St Stephen Museum in Székesfehérvár; the two are likely to have been made in the same workshop. In Hungary, many such crucifixes were found in churches destroyed during the Tatar invasion in 1241.

9 Throne Carpet

Made in Florence during the Renaissance at the request of King Mátyás, the throne carpet *(below)* carries the coat of arms of Mátyás, Hungary and Dalmatia, and the raven of the Hunyadi family. This is the only one of its kind remaining in Hungary.

10 Campaigning in Front of the National Museum

As the title suggests, this pre-Secession painting by Friedrich Weiss depicts the political campaigning of reformists and conservatives between 1847 and 1848. It illustrates the fact that art forms in that period tended to depict great events.

Ferenc and István Széchenyi

It is uncertain whether the National Museum would have existed at all without the vast collection of art and artifacts donated in 1802 by Count Ferenc Széchényi, who also established the National Library. His equally illustrious son, Count István Széchenyi, is regarded as one of the greatest Hungarians. An aristocratic polymath, István wrote several treatises for the upliftment of peasants, advocated land reform, dabbled in revolutionary politics and even paid for the country's first railway, from Pest to Vác.

Statue Park and Memento Park

A visit to Statue Park takes you back in time to an age when the Communists ruled half of Europe and artists had to conform to the whims of a committee. The result was some of the most striking sculpture of the 20th century, preserved in a bizarre theme park. While most of the Soviet bloc destroyed its socialist statuary after the fall of the Communist regime, the Hungarians decided to preserve these works of art. The park was recently enlarged to include Memento Park.

Statue of Lenin at entrance

Statue Park is a 20-minute drive from Central Pest. There are direct buses from Deák ter at 11am daily. A combined bus and entrance ticket costs Ft3,950, and can be purchased from the Statue Park kiosk or on the bus.

- *Map N3*
- *XXII, south Buda, corner of Balatoni út and Szabadkai utca*
- *424 75 00*
- *Open 10am–dusk daily*
- *Adm Ft1,500*
- *www.szoborpark.hu*

Top 10 Attractions

1. Main Entrance
2. Karl Marx and Frederick Engels
3. Béla Kun Memorial
4. Hungarian-Soviet Friendship Memorial
5. Republic of Councils Monument
6. Captain Steinmetz
7. Lenin
8. Georgi Dimitrov
9. Worker's Movement Memorial
10. Souvenir Shop

1 Main Entrance

Although the Iron Curtain is a thing of the past, the austere wall that surrounds Statue Park is a reminder of how divisive it used to be. The archway on the left-hand side of the main entrance *(above)* shelters a statue of Lenin.

2 Karl Marx and Frederick Engels

The authors of the *Communist Manifesto* stand next to each other *(right)* under a large arch on the right-hand side of the entrance. Note how Engels is slightly behind – and in the shadow of – Marx, reflecting his role in life as the younger of the two.

3 Béla Kun Memorial

In 1919, the Hungarian Communist Béla Kun briefly ran the country, but was overthrown by Admiral Horthy. He fled to Russia and died in Stalin's purges.

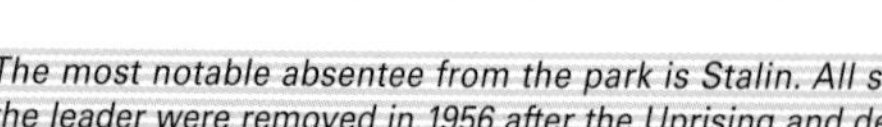

The most notable absentee from the park is Stalin. All statues of the leader were removed in 1956 after the Uprising and destroyed.

4 Hungarian-Soviet Friendship Memorial

There was never much amity between the Soviet Union, viewed as an occupying force, and Hungary, but this statue *(right)* of a Hungarian worker greeting a Red Army soldier would like us to think otherwise.

7 Lenin

There are three Lenin statues in the park. The one of him clutching the *Manifesto* in one hand is the most resonant.

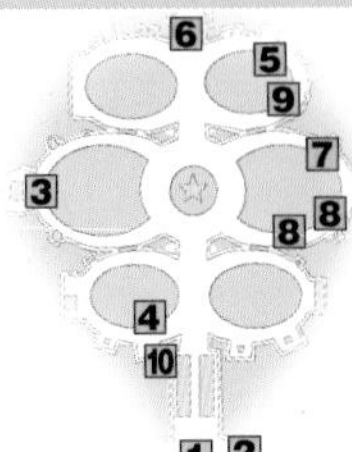

9 Worker's Movement Memorial

This sculpture of two large hands about to clasp a globe *(below)* symbolizes the working classes being on the verge of grasping the world in their hands and creating a utopian paradise.

Hungarian Fighters, Spanish International Brigades Memorial

5 Republic of Councils Monument

This massive, 10-m (30-ft) high statue almost makes you want to leap up and launch your own revolution. It was designed to call the working classes to arms in order to defend Hungary against foreign aggressors.

6 Captain Steinmetz

In 1945, Captain Miklós Steinmetz (right) was sent by the Russian army to offer terms of surrender to the Nazis. The Germans, however, curtly dismissed him, and he was killed while returning to Soviet lines.

8 Georgi Dimitrov

The park features two statues of Georgi Dimitrov, leader of the Bulgarian Communist Party from 1945 to 1949.

10 Souvenir Shop

You could spend a fortune in this capitalist shrine to Communism, which sells mementos from all over the Soviet bloc, including reproduction Soviet army watches, Trabant keyrings and CDs of rousing Communist anthems.

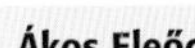

Ákos Eleőd

The layout of Statue Park is not haphazard. In fact, it was carefully designed and planned by the architect Ákos Eleőd, who wished to create an "anti-propaganda" theme park. As he explained in his own words: "it may be a park dedicated to dictatorship, but the fact it is here, that it can be talked about and discussed implies that it is also a park about democracy."

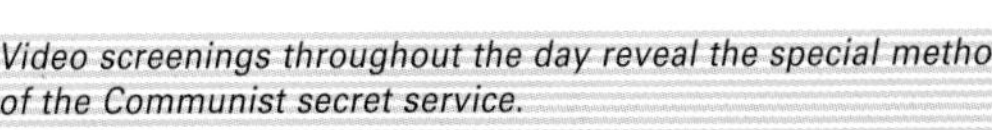

Video screenings throughout the day reveal the special methods of the Communist secret service.

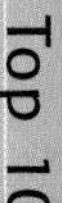

Left **Magyar invasion** Centre **Budapest ghetto** Right **Hungary becomes a republic, 1989**

Top 10 Moments in History

1 AD 409: Huns Conquer Aquincum

Established in the area that now lies on the city's northern periphery, Aquincum *(see p95)* was an important town and military garrison in the Roman province of Pannonia. It was conquered by the Huns in 409, and subsequently ruled by the Goths, the Longobards and the Avars.

2 896: Árpád Leads the Magyars into Pannonia

Prince Árpád led the nomadic Magyars – tribes who originated in the Urals and inhabited an area east of the River Tisza – into Pannonia in 896. He settled first on Csepel Island, in the middle of the Danube in southern Budapest, and later in Óbuda (meaning Ancient Buda in Hungarian).

3 1000: Stephen I Crowned King

Stephen (István) was the first Magyar to accept Christianity, and for doing so, the pope crowned him king. He cemented the Árpád dynasty, which lasted a further 300 years.

4 1687: The Beginning of the Age of the Habsburgs

The Habsburgs became rulers of Hungary more by stealth than conquest. They completed their takeover in 1687, when the Hungarians gave up their right to elect their king, and ceded the crown to the Habsburg Empire. In one guise or another, they ruled Hungary until 1918.

5 1849: Chain Bridge Links Buda and Pest

The first permanent bridge over the Danube, the Chain Bridge was designed by the Englishman William Tierney Clark, and built by a Scotsman, Adam Clark. Its completion in 1849 allowed the unification of Buda, Óbuda and Pest some 20 years later.

Emperor Franz József I (1830–1916)

6 1916: Charles IV Crowned Last King of Hungary

On the death of Emperor Franz József in 1916, Charles IV was crowned king of Hungary. He abdicated in November 1918, and despite attempting to regain the throne in 1919 after the defeat of Béla Kun's Communists, he was exiled to Madeira, Portugal, where he died in 1922.

7 1944: The Budapest Ghetto

In 1944, the Nazi regime and their Hungarian allies, the Arrow Cross, herded over 70,000 Jews into the area around the Great Synagogue *(see p84)*. Though well over 20,000 Jews perished, 50,000 survived and were liberated by the Soviet army in February 1945.

8 1956: The Hungarian Uprising

Following mass anti-Soviet demonstrations in October 1956, the Hungarian Communist Party's Central Committee elected the popular Imre Nagy as prime minister. On 4 November, however, just 18 days after he assumed office, the Soviet army invaded Hungary and crushed the new regime. Nagy was arrested and executed in 1958.

9 1989: The People's Republic Comes to a Peaceful End

Anticipating the changes that would eventually sweep the whole of Eastern Europe, Communist authorities in Hungary sanctioned the creation of opposition political parties in February 1989. The People's Republic of Hungary became the Republic of Hungary in October, and in January 1990, free elections were held for the first time since 1919.

10 2004: Hungary Joins the European Union

After ten years of negotiations, Hungary became a full member of the European Union on 1 June 2004. The occasion was marked with days of celebrations throughout the country, and was greeted positively by most of the population. Hungary had previously become a member of NATO in 1999.

Celebrating EU membership on Chain Bridge

Top 10 Great Hungarians

1 Ödön Lechner (1845–1914)

Groundbreaking Secessionist architect, often considered as the father of the Secession Movement *(see p23)*.

2 Sándor Petőfi (1823–49)

Nationalist poet whose recital of his poem *Nemzeti Dal* (National Song) and the 12 pont (12 points) on the steps of the National Museum in 1848 sparked a revolt *(see p30)*.

3 János Vaszary (1867–1939)

Leading exponent of Secessionist painting, whose works can be seen at the National Gallery *(see pp20–23)*.

4 Ferenc (Franz) Liszt (1811–86)

Hungarian composer, regarded by many as the best pianist of all time.

5 István Szabó (b. 1938)

Film director who received an Oscar for his film *Mephisto* in 1981.

6 László Bíró (1899–1985)

Eccentric journalist who invented the world's first ball-point pen in 1939.

7 Ferenc Puskás (1927–2006)

Footballer who led the great Hungarian team of the 1950s *(see p96)*.

8 Miklós Ybl (1814–91)

Architect whose work includes the peerless State Opera House *(see pp26–7)*.

9 Mihály Vörösmarty (1800–55)

19th-century poet and author of the epic *The Flight of Zalán*.

10 Attila József (1905–37)

Radical poet who wrote of love and despair.

Begun among artists in Paris and Vienna in the 1880s, the Secession Movement's hallmark was its colourful, often fantastical designs.

Exterior of the Széchenyi Baths, the biggest bathing complex in Europe

TOP 10 Baths and Swimming Pools

Indoor pool at the Gellért Baths

1 Gellért Hotel and Baths

Of all Budapest's many baths, the finest are those at the splendid Gellért Hotel, open to non-residents every day of the year. The outdoor pools feature one of the world's first artificial wave machines *(see pp16–17)*.

2 Széchenyi Baths

Set in a stunning Secession building in Városliget Park, the Széchenyi Baths offer a full range of thermal water treatments. The complex has a number of outdoor and indoor pools *(see p89)*.

3 Rudas Baths

The Rudas Baths are among the oldest in the city, they were built in an opulent style by the Turks in the 16th century. *Map K5 • I, Döbrentei tér 9 • 356 13 22 • Open men: 6am–8pm Mon, Wed–Fri; women: 6am–8pm Tue; both: 10pm–4am Fri, 6am–4am Sat, 6am–5pm Sun • Adm Ft1,900 • www.budapestspas.hu*

4 Lukács Baths

Opened in 1894, the Neo-Classical Lukács Baths offer two outdoor swimming pools, busy in summer, and a large indoor thermal pool. Mud baths are also available. *Map B2 • II, Frankel Leó út 25–9 • 326 16 95 • Undergoing renovation work so check opening times first • Adm Ft2,500 (with cabin), Ft2,100 (with locker) • www.budapestspas.hu*

5 Király Baths

Another of the city's original Turkish baths, the Király Baths opened in 1566 for Pasha Arslan, an Ottoman governor. The pools, steam rooms and saunas are centred on a sensational central dome and octagonal pool. *Map B3 • II, Fő utca 82–4 • 202 36 88 • Open 7am–6pm Mon, Wed, Fri (women only), 9am–8pm Tue, Thu, Sat (men only) • Adm Ft1,600 • www.budapestspas.hu*

6 Hajós Alfréd Pool

Designed by Hajós Alfréd, who represented Hungary at the 1896 Olympic Games in swimming and football, the three sports pools (including an Olympic-size one) are still used by the Hungarian swimming team for training. *Map B1 • XIII, Margaret Island • 450 42 00 • Open 6am–4pm Mon–Fri, 6am–6pm Sat & Sun • Adm Ft1,500*

Ottoman domes at the Király Baths

Most of Budapest's baths have separate bathing areas for men and women, a tradition dating back to the time the Turks built them.

Swimming pool at Palatinus Strand

7 Palatinus Strand

Budapest's most popular swimming complex has water slides, pools of all sizes and hot springs, all set amidst the peace and tranquillity of Margaret Island. *Map P1 • XIII, Margaret Island • 340 45 05 • Open May–Sep: 9am–7pm daily • Adm*

8 Rácz Baths

Recognized as a UNESCO World Heritage Site, the Rácz Baths still retain a glorious 15th-century Ottoman dome and octagonal pool. They form part of the luxury, five-star spa hotel complex, Baglioni Hotel.The baths are open to day visitors. *Map J5 • I, Hadnagy út 8–10 • 225 12 75*

9 Dagály Medicinal Baths and Strand

Some way from the city centre, the Dagály Strand is Budapest's largest pool complex, with 12 pools including children's pools and a hydrotherapy and fitness centre. *Map P1 • XIII, Népfürdő út 36 • 452 45 00 • Open 6am–7pm Mon–Fri, 6am–5pm Sat & Sun • Adm*

10 Danubius Grand Hotel Margitsziget

Budapest's most exclusive baths are those at the equally exclusive Danubius Grand Hotel Margitsziget. Don't be at all surprised if you find a Hollywood star sharing the hot tub with you *(see p113)*.

Top 10 Bath Tips

1 Etiquette
Many of the more traditional thermal baths still insist on separate pools for men and women. In such cases, swimming costumes are not usually worn.

2 Payment
The price list, posted in Hungarian, German and English at the entrance to all the baths, usually runs to several pages. Basic entrance, valid for up to four hours, is usually all you will need.

3 Towels
Bring your own. Towels can be hired, but are expensive and not altogether soft.

4 Bathrobes
In single-sex baths, you will be handed a small sheet as a matter of course.

5 Lockers
Most baths have secure lockers where you can leave valuables for a small fee.

6 Water Temperature
In all baths, the temperature of the water is clearly displayed by the side of the pool.

7 Steam Rooms
Entrance to the steam room – where there is one – is usually included in the standard entrance fee.

8 Massage
Almost all baths and pools offer various forms of massage at extra cost.

9 Wave Pools
Gellért, Dagály and Palatinus Strand all have artificial wave machines.

10 Family Bathing
Children are welcome in all the city's baths. Note, though, that families wishing to bathe together should head to a non-segregated bath.

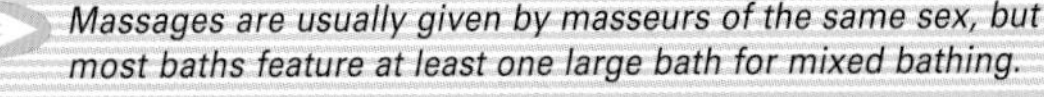
Massages are usually given by masseurs of the same sex, but most baths feature at least one large bath for mixed bathing.

Left **National Gallery** Centre **National Museum façade** Right **Sword of László, National Museum**

TOP 10 Museums and Galleries

1 Hungarian National Gallery

More than 10,000 exhibits make the National Gallery's collection one of the greatest in the world. Spread over much of the Royal Palace, every significant Hungarian work of art from medieval times to the present day is displayed here *(see pp20–23)*.

2 Hungarian National Museum

Founded on the personal collection of philanthropist Count Ferenc Széchenyi, the National Museum has been home to a stunning array of Hungarian artifacts since 1802. The building is a masterpiece in its own right *(see pp30–31)*.

3 Museum of Fine Arts

If the Neo-Classical building that houses the Museum of Fine Arts doesn't overwhelm you, step inside to enjoy the fine collection of pieces from all artistic eras and genres. Raphael, Toulouse-Lautrec, Picasso and Goya all feature, and there are also collections of ancient Egyptian and Greek art *(see p89)*.

Brixen's *Birth of Mary*, Museum of Fine Arts

4 Budapest History Museum

In a rather haphazard but nevertheless gripping manner, the Budapest History Museum tells the story of the city from the Middle Ages till today. This museum is at its best when it recounts the story of the Royal Castle and Palace, in which it is housed *(see p63)*.

5 Jewish Museum

Budapest's proud Jewish community is based around Europe's largest synagogue – the Great Synagogue. Next door is the community's museum, established in 1931 and still home to thousands of Jewish historic relics and devotional items. There is also a room devoted to the Holocaust, while in the courtyard there is a memorial to the 600,000 Hungarian Jews killed by the Nazis. *Map M4 • VII, Dohány utca 2 • 342 89 49 • Open Mar–Oct: 10am–5:30pm Sun–Thu, 10am–2:30pm Fri; Nov–Apr: 10am–5:30pm Sun–Thu, 10am–1:30pm Fri • Adm • www.greatsynagogue.hu*

6 Museum of Applied Arts

Don't miss the Oriental rugs, nor the Zsolnay ceramics or Secessionist furniture in this

Zsolnay ceiling tiles, Museum of Applied Arts

outstanding museum. First opened in 1896 for Budapest's Millennium Celebrations, it is housed in a superb Secessionist building designed by Ödön Lechner *(see p84).*

7 Vasarely Museum

Born Győző Vásárhelyi, Victor Vasarely carved himself a place in art history as the founder of the Op-Art movement in Paris in the 1930s. A museum dedicated to his life and work, featuring almost 500 pieces, is based in Zichy Palace in Óbuda. *Map P1 • III, Szentlélek tér 6 • 388 75 51 • Open 10am–5:30pm Tue–Sun*

8 Ethnographical Museum

Not without its charms, including a fine collection of costumes and uniforms from throughout Hungary's history, this is one museum where the building far outweighs the exhibits. Designed by Alajos Hauszmann and built in 1893–6. *Map K1 • V, Kossuth Lajos tér 12 • 473 24 00 • Open 10am–6pm Tue–Sun • Dis. access at the Szalay utca entrance • Adm • www.neprajz.hu*

9 Ludwig Museum Budapest – Museum of Contemporary Art

If the splendour of Empire and the Secession become too much for you, head for this museum for a bewildering display of modern Hungarian art. More than 150 works from 1960 onwards document the progression of Hungarian artists as they attempted to break out of Socialist Realism. There are also a number of works by international contemporary artists. *Map P2 • IX, Palace of Arts, Komor Marcell utca 1 • 555 34 44 • Open 10am–8pm Tue–Sun, 10am–10pm last Sat of the month • Adm • www.ludwigmuseum.hu*

10 Museum of Military History

Uniforms, flags, maps, weapons and photographs document the many battles that have been fought over Budapest. The museum is especially effective when it tells the story of the 1956 National Uprising, and of the many Hungarians who subsequently lost their lives in the repression that followed. *Map A3 • I, Tóth Árpád sétány 40 • 325 16 51 • Open 10am–6pm Tue–Sun*

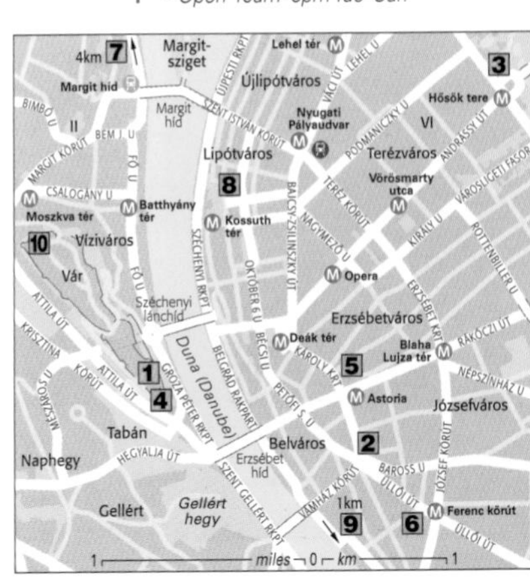

Left **St Stephen's Basilica** Centre **Rose window, Mátyás Church** Right **Interior, Cave Church**

TOP 10 Places of Worship

1 St Stephen's Basilica

The grandest of Budapest's many spectacular churches is fittingly named after the country's first king, St Stephen. Built in the latter part of the 19th century, it dominates the city skyline and can be seen from most parts of Budapest *(see pp12–13)*.

2 Mátyás Church

Mátyás Church has been a piece of Budapest history since the 13th century. It has been the stage for a number of seminal events, including the marriage of King Mátyás, and the coronations of Franz József I in 1867 and Charles IV in 1916 *(see pp24–5)*.

3 Great Synagogue

Completed in 1859, this is the largest synagogue in Europe. Its design betrays the desire of 19th-century Jews to assimilate into Hungarian society. The twin towers, for example, are clearly inspired by Christian church steeples. During World War II, the synagogue was used as a detention centre and also acted as the centre of the Budapest ghetto *(see p84)*.

Figure of St Florian, Inner City Parish Church

4 Cave Church

The remarkable Cave Church was built into Gellért Hill by Pauline monks following a pilgrimage to Lourdes. It was consecrated on Whit Sunday 1926. Bricked up during the Communist period, it reopened in August 1989 *(see p69)*.

5 Inner City Parish Church

Almost destroyed to make way for Elizabeth Bridge *(see p42)* when it was being rebuilt after World War II, the Inner City Parish Church was miraculously saved when the builders had a last-minute change of heart. The oldest building in Pest, dating from the 14th century, it was damaged by fire in 1723 and rebuilt by György Pauer in 1725–39. Don't miss the vaulted Gothic chapel *(see p83)*.

6 St Anne's Church

The twin-towered parish church of Víziváros is one of the most beautiful Baroque churches in Hungary. Built from 1740 to 1805, its highlights include the painted ceiling by Gergely Vogl, the high altar and

Splendid Baroque interior, St Anne's Church

the magnificent Baroque pulpit. ✆ *Map H1 • I, Batthyány tér 7 • 201 34 04 • Open 10am–10pm daily*

7 Capuchin Church

Just a short walk along Fő utca from St Anne's Church lies the charming Capuchin Church, a 19th-century replica of an earlier building. The first church on the site was founded in the 14th century, but was converted into a mosque during the Turkish occupation and almost entirely destroyed in 1686. Of the few original features to remain is the doorway on the southern façade. ✆ *Map H2 • I, Fő utca 32 • 201 47 25 • Open 10:15–11:45am Tue–Fri (also open by prior arrangement)*

8 Serbian Church

Built by Serbian settlers in 1698, this Baroque church replaced an earlier one on the same site. The church's interior is arranged according to the Greek Orthodox tradition, as the Serbs follow the Orthodox liturgy. The iconostasis that surrounds the choir gallery and divides it from the sanctuary dates from 1850. It was carved by Serb sculptor Mihai Janic. ✆ *Map L5 • V, Szerb utca 2–4 • Open 8am–7pm daily*

9 Lutheran Church

This striking church is characterized by its utter simplicity, in keeping with the design of most Protestant churches throughout Central Europe. Built between 1797 and 1808, it is not without charm, though its very ordinariness is what makes it stand out. Superb acoustics make it a popular venue for classical and organ concerts. ✆ *Map L3 • V, Deák tér 5 • 235 02 07 • Open 10am–6pm Tue–Sun*

10 Franciscan Church

Built originally in the 13th century, the Franciscan Church – like many churches in Budapest – was used as a mosque during the Turkish occupation in the 16th and 17th centuries. It was rebuilt by the Franciscan order between 1727 and 1743, and their emblem remains visible today in the main portal. Numerous sculptures of Franciscan saints also decorate the church's façade. ✆ *Map L4 • V, Ferenciek tere 9 • 317 33 22 • Open 6am–noon, 4pm–7:45pm daily*

Painting by Károly Lotz, Franciscan Church

Left **The Chain Bridge** Centre **Cruise boat** Right **Sculpture by Adolphe Thabart, Margaret Bridge**

TOP 10 Danube Sights

1 Chain Bridge

Completed in 1849, the Chain Bridge (Széchenyi Lánchíd) was the first permanent crossing between Buda and Pest. On either side of the Bridge are two huge towers that support the mammoth chains from which the bridge takes its name. The towers are superbly lit at night, which makes the bridge one of the city's most photographed sights. In summer, the bridge closes at weekends to host a cultural festival *(see p49)*. ✎ *Map J3*

2 River Cruises

A number of companies run tours along the Danube during the summer, beginning from Vigadó tér. Mahart Passnave run evening cruises – including drinks and dinner – every day from May to September. There are also daily hydrofoil services to Bratislava and Vienna from April to November. ✎ *Mahart Passnave: Map K4; V, Vigadó tér, Dock 5–6; 318 12 23, 484 40 13; www.mahartpassnave.hu*

3 Elizabeth Bridge

The longest suspension bridge in the world when completed in 1903, Elizabeth Bridge (Erzsébet híd) had to be completely rebuilt after World War II, and did not reopen until 1963. Great care had to be taken on the Pest side to ensure that the Inner City Parish Church *(see p83)* was not damaged during rebuilding; indeed at one stage the church's continued existence was threatened, with the builders and the Communist authorities wanting to demolish it. A compromise was reached however, and today the roadway passes just inches from the church's walls. ✎ *Map K5*

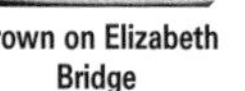

Crown on Elizabeth Bridge

4 Hungarian Parliament

The city's number one sight looks better from the water or from the opposite bank of the Danube than from anywhere else. The splendour of its startling design – based on Britain's Parliament building – is only enhanced by the river's soothing effect *(see pp8–11)*.

5 Margaret Island

Budapest's oasis and a great place to spend summer afternoons, Margaret Island was in fact three separate islands until

View of the Parliament from across the Danube

For more information on river boat cruises **see p104.**

The elegant Margaret Bridge

they were joined together by ground-breaking embankment work in the latter part of the 19th century *(see pp18–19)*.

6 Margaret Bridge

The gateway to Margaret Island, Margit híd was built by a Frenchman, Ernest Gouin, from 1872 to 1876, and is distinguished by its unusual chevron shape. The approach road to the island, however, was actually an embarrassing afterthought, and wasn't added until the 1890s. *Map B2*

7 Academy of Sciences

The historicist Academy actually stands in Roosevelt tér facing the square, not the river, but its superb Neo-Classical faćade can be admired by anyone travelling upstream, while the aspect that faces the Danube is no less impressive. Built from 1862 to 1864, it was designed by architect Friedrich August Stüler *(see p76)*.

8 Liberty Bridge

Legendary Hungarian *tural* birds sit atop the Modernist, bold girders of Liberty Bridge (Szabadság híd). First constructed in 1894–99, it was entirely rebuilt after being destroyed by the Nazis during World War II, and is an exact replica of the original. It was earlier known as Emperor Franz József Bridge, but the Communists unsurprisingly decided on a less imperial name. *Map L6*

9 Embankment Walk

This walk extends along most of the Pest embankment, from Liberty Bridge to Margaret Island and beyond. Several boats moored on the various quays have cafés aboard, including Columbus, one of the city's best *(see p54)*, and Spoon, one of the newest in Budapest. *Map B3, B4, C5 • Spoon Café & Lounge: V, Vigadó tér 3, Port; 411 09 33; Open noon–midnight daily; www.spooncafe.hu*

10 Buda Castle Funicular

Kids of all ages love to ride up and down the archaic funicular. The journey is short, the cabins tiny, but the views of the Danube below are superb. Also, on a chilly, windy or rainy day, it sure beats walking up to the castle. *Map H3 • I, Buda Castle, Clark Ádam tér • 201 91 28 • Open 7:30am–10pm; closed 1st and 3rd Mon of every month • Adm*

Left **Budapest circus emblem** Right **Labyrinth of Budavár**

Top 10 Children's Attractions

1 Cogwheel Railway and Children's Railway

Children between the ages of 9 and 14 man a narrow-gauge railway that runs through the Buda Hills *(see p95)* from Széchenyi Hill to Hűvös Valley. The only adults on board are the engineers. To get to the train, you first have to take the cog railway from Városmajor station up to the top of Széchenyi Hill. This track is 3,730 m (12,240 ft) long and climbs to 315 m (1,035 ft). *Cogwheel Railway: Map N1, N2; II, Városmajor station, Szilágyi Erzsébet fasor 47; 355 41 67; open 5am–11pm daily; Adm • Children's Railway: Map N2, N1; XII, Golfpalya út; 397 53 92; open 9am–4pm daily (timings of last the trains vary); Adm*

2 Funicular

Children love riding in the front cabin of the Budapest Castle funicular. The journey takes just a minute or so, but the views of the Danube as you climb up to the Castle are magnificent *(see also p43)*.

Cycling along the shores of the Boating Lake

3 Transport Museum

A fine collection of trains, buses, trams, bicycles, helicopters and planes is on display at this museum. Children are allowed to clamber over many of the exhibits. *Map F2 • XIV, Városliget (City Park) • 273 38 40 • Open 10am–5pm Tue–Fri (4pm in winter), 10am–6pm Sat & Sun (5pm in winter) • Adm*

4 Palatinus Strand

Margaret Island is home to Palatinus Strand, Budapest's most popular swimming pool and thermal bath complex. Slides and a variety of children's pools make it a popular choice for families *(see p37)*.

5 Open-Air Skating Rink and Boating Lake

In winter, Városliget Lake turns into a superb skating rink, where people of all ages skate to classical music. During the summer, boats replace the skaters as families row their craft around the lake. Skates and boats can be hired at the jetty near the pavilion. *Városliget (City Park): Map E2; Budapest XIV • Boating Lake: Olof Palme sétány 5; 364 00 13; currently closed for reconstruction • Skating Rink: open 20 Oct–4 Mar: 9am–1pm, 4–8pm Mon–Fri, 10am–2pm, 4–8pm Sat & Sun; Adm*

6 Circus

This permanent circus offers great performances every day of the week except Monday and

Circus building façade

Tuesday when it's closed. The programme varies, but there are always plenty of clowns, animals and acrobats, often from well-known visiting troupes. In summer, the circus hosts the International Circus Festival. *Map E1 • XIV, Városliget (City Park), Állatkerti körút 7 • 344 60 08 • Daily performances at 3pm except on Mon & Tue • Adm*

7 Budapest Zoo

Budapest's zoo is large, well funded and one of the best in the region. It has a large aquarium, an impressive aviary, and a superb reptile house. The staff speak several languages and help children feel involved *(see p91)*.

8 Funfair

Established in 1878, Városliget's slightly old-fashioned funfair still has enough rides to keep the kids happy for hours. Older children can take pot shots at moving targets on the shooting range. *Map E1 • XIV, Városliget (City Park), Állatkerti körút 14–16 • 363 83 10 • Open Apr–mid-Sep: 10am–8pm daily; mid-Sep–Oct: noon–6:30pm Mon–Fri, 10am–6:30pm Sat & Sun • Adm • www.vidampark.hu*

9 Planetarium

Although small and by no means spectacular, Budapest's planetarium accurately charts the course of the planets and the stars, accompanied by a slightly dated pop and rock soundtrack. With shows throughout the day, it is another good rainy day option. *Map P2 • X, Népliget • 263 18 11 • Open 9am–4pm Tue–Sun • Adm • www.planetarium.hu*

10 Labyrinth of Budavár

Make sure you don't lose your kids in this underground maze of tunnels and chambers. It is believed that these caves were formed by hot springs about half a million years ago. The music and bizarre exhibits somewhat detract from the historical importance of the place – it was a refuge for hunters and gatherers from around 10,000 BC, and served as a bomb shelter during World War II – but it's still worth a visit. *Map G2, G3 • I, Úri utca 9 • 489 32 80 • Open 9:30am–7:30pm daily • Adm • www.labirintus.com*

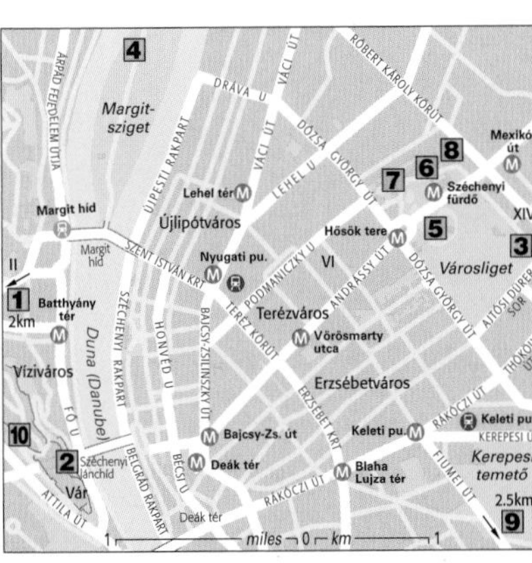

Left **Opening ceremony of the Spring Festival, Heroes' Square** Right **Adam's *Giselle*, BudaFest**

Festivals and Events

1 Spring Festival

Budapest's Spring Festival runs for three weeks in March and April and features world-class performers. Outstanding opera, chamber and classical music, literature and theatre take over almost every performance art venue in the city. *www.festivalcity.hu*

Spring Festival logo

2 BudaFest

Every July and August since 1992, the State Opera House, the Hilton Dominican Court and St Stephen's Basilica have hosted the BudaFest Summer Music Festival. The festival plays host to the most distinguished tenors, sopranos and ballet soloists, as well as jazz and folk musicians and contemporary dancers. *www.viparts.hu*

3 Hungarian Arts and Crafts Festival

Each year in August, Disz tér in the Castle District comes alive for four days of arts and crafts. Skilled craftsmen from all over Hungary flock here to display and sell their wares. There are also performances of Hungarian folk music and dancing. The highlight, however, is the craftsmen's parade on St Stephen's Day (20 August).

4 Sziget Festival

Central Europe's biggest pop and rock festival makes perfect use of Óbudai, an island in the middle of the Danube. The world's leading artistes perform over a week in mid-August. Most revellers stay on the island the whole week, sleeping in tents. *www.sziget.hu*

5 Budapest Búcsú Festival

Held on the last weekend in June, this festival celebrates the withdrawal of the last Soviet soldier from Hungary in 1991. Concerts and events are held throughout the city, a lot of them outdoors, and there is also a carnival. *www.festivalcity.hu*

6 Bridge Festival

Every mid-June the historic Chain Bridge is closed for a day to celebrate its anniversary. All kinds of events and activities are staged on the bridge, by the bridge and along the banks, from brass bands to theatrical performances. There are also races held on the river. The festival is brought to a close with floating candles and a firework display. *www.festivalcity.hu*

Shopping at the Arts and Crafts Festival

Previous pages: **River view of Chain Bridge & St Stephen's Basilica**

Ferrari technicians, Hungarian Grand Prix

7 Hungarian Grand Prix

The Hungaroring circuit, 19 km (12 miles) from Budapest, is one of the most exciting circuits on the Formula One calendar. The city goes into full Grand Prix mode at least a week before race weekend (usually at the end of July). Tickets are expensive and best booked in advance. *www.hungaroring.hu*

8 Jewish Summer Festival

This week-long celebration of Jewish culture is usually held at the end of August. It features music, dance, visual arts, comedy and cabaret. Full details are available at the Jewish Museum *(see p38)*. *www.jewishfestival.hu*

9 Summer on Chain Bridge

Arts replace cars on the Chain Bridge every Saturday and Sunday from the first weekend in July to mid-August. Painters, musicians, dancers and even a brass band or jazz orchestra entertain the large crowds.

Hungarian red wine

10 Budapest Wine Festival

Every September, Buda Castle provides the perfect location for Hungary's fiercely competitive wine producers and gastronomes to display their latest creations and vintages. *www.winefestival.hu*

Top 10 National Holidays

1 St Stephen's Day (20 Aug)
Celebrates the coronation of St Stephen (István), Hungary's patron saint with a firework display over the Danube.

2 Christmas (25 Dec)
The city's famed Christmas gift market is held every December in Vörösmarty tér.

3 New Year (31 Dec)
New Year's Eve is celebrated on the streets. Vörösmarty tér usually hosts pop concerts and firework displays.

4 Anniversary of 1848 Revolution (15 Mar)
Hungarians pay their respects to Sándor Petőfi by re-enacting his poem and 12 *ponts* (points) at the Hungarian National Museum *(see pp30–31)*.

5 Easter (Mar/Apr)
A devoutly Catholic people, Hungarians celebrate Easter quietly, usually at home.

6 Labour Day (1 May)
Once a Communist holiday marked with military processions, Labour Day is still observed as a national holiday.

7 Whit Sunday (7th Sunday after Easter)
National holiday celebrating the descent of the Holy Spirit.

8 Withdrawal of the Red Army (19 Jun)
Though not a national holiday, the withdrawal of the Red Army from Hungary in 1991 is still marked by many people.

9 Republic Day (23 Oct)
A double celebration marks the outbreak of the 1956 revolution and the 1989 proclamation of the Republic of Hungary.

10 All Saints' Day (1 Nov)
Celebrates saints who do not have their own holy days.

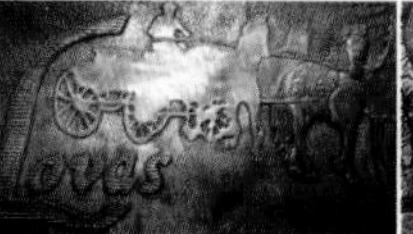

Left **WestEnd City Center** Centre **Nagy Lovas sign** Right **Sausages on sale, Central Market Hall**

Top 10 Shops and Markets

1 WestEnd City Center

This vast, three-level complex of more than 400 shops is next to Nyugati Railway Station. All your favourite brands and stores can be found here, though don't expect bargains, as prices are often higher than at home. Don't miss the rooftop garden and balloon ride. *Map C2 • VI, Váci út 1–3 • 238 77 77 • Open (shops) 10am–9pm Mon–Sat, 10am–6pm Sun • Dis. access*

2 Central Market Hall

Budapest's main produce market is great for local delicacies. Impeccably clean, it has numerous stalls selling meat, salami, fruit and vegetables. The upper floor has a small café and souvenir stalls. *Map M6 • V, Vámház körút 1–3 • 366 34 97 • Open 6am–5pm Mon, 6am–6pm Tue–Fri, 6am–2pm Sat • Dis. access*

Fruit and vegetable stalls, Central Market Hall

3 Apponyi Márkabolt

As much a museum as it is a shop, Apponyi is an authorized retailer of Hungary's finest porcelain, known as Herend. The Herend factory, to the west of the city, has been making exquisite porcelain for generations. Most pieces at Apponyi command high prices. Everything is displayed in large wooden cabinets – themselves priceless – beneath a splendid wooden ceiling. *Map K3 • V, József nádor tér 11 • 317 26 22 • Open 10am–6pm Mon–Fri, 10am–2pm Sat*

4 Nagy Lovas

Hungary is renowned for its horses and Hungarians for their horsemanship. This fabulous shop is equally famous for its range of equestrian gear – saddles, bridles, riding boots, gloves, canes and whips. No bargains are on offer; just excellent quality products. *Map D5 • VIII, József körút 69 • 338 25 55 • Open 9am–5pm Mon–Fri, 9am–1pm Sat • www.nagylovas.hu*

5 Folkart Centrum

Hungarian arts and crafts that are brought directly from the countryside are sold here. You'll find a fine selection of embroidery, textiles, carpets, ceramics, porcelain, dolls, woodcarvings, jewellery and dresses. The shop will also ensure the packing and shipping of your purchases if they are too large for you to carry. *Map L5 • V, Váci utca 58 • 318 58 40 • Open 10am–7pm daily*

Most shops open between 9–10am in the morning and close between 5–7pm Mon–Fri. Many shops stay open on weekends; timings vary.

Souvenirs at the Flea Market

6 Flea Market

Fortunately, EU membership hasn't yet led to the demise of Budapest's eclectic flea markets, where anything and everything is on sale. The best market is in the centre of the city's largest park, Városliget (City Park), where you can pick up anything from Soviet memorabilia to second-hand records, ethnic art and crafts, as well as coins, medals and weapons. *Map F2 • XIV, Zichy Mihály utca 14, Városliget • 348 32 01 • Open 7am–2pm Sat & Sun*

7 Bonbon Delicatesse

There is more to this marvellous delicatessen than just confectionery and chocolates. It sells a full range of Hungarian foodstuff including salami, pâté, spirits and wines and remains open well past midnight. *Map K3 • V, Váci utca 11/b • 488 72 46 • Open 9am–9pm daily*

8 BÁV Jewellery (Rubin Ékszerbolt)

A collection of fine antique watches and jewellery from one of Hungary's best known auction houses. There are several other BÁV shops across the city, all with different specializations. The outlets on Kossuth Lajos utca deal in art and porcelain. *BÁV Jewellery: Map L4; V, Párizsi utca 2; 318 62 17 • BÁV: Map M4; V, Bécsi utca 1; 266 20 87 • Open (both shops) 10am–6pm Mon–Fri, 10am–2pm Sat • www.bav.hu*

9 Polgár Galeria

A sensational art and antiques gallery where you can purchase works by classical and contemporary Hungarian artists. You will also find rare antiques, including imperial Habsburg furniture. The gallery also looks after all onward shipping and related paperwork. *Map M4 • V, Kossuth Lajos utca 3 • 318 69 54 • Open 10am–6pm Mon–Fri, 10am–1pm Sat*

10 Rózsavölgyi Zeneműbolt

Hungary's best record store is located over two floors of a large space opposite the City Hall. Classical music is on the ground floor, including works by all the country's greatest composers. Pop and rock fans should head for the basement. *Map L4 • V, Szervita tér 5 • 318 35 00 • Open 9:30am–7pm Mon, Tue, Thu, Fri, 10am–7pm Wed, 10am–5pm Sat*

For shopping tips see p107.

Left **Sign for Jazz Garden** Centre **Búsulo Juhász Étterem** Right **Onyx Restaurant**

Top 10 Restaurants

1 Kacsa

Kacsa means "duck" in Hungarian, so it's easy to guess what dominates the menu here. Duck is served in many inventive guises, created by a brilliant chef. There is more than duck on offer, however, and the wine list is simply superb. *Map B3 • I, Fő utca 75 • 201 99 92 • Open noon–midnight • Dis. access • www.kacsavendeglo.hu • FFFFF*

2 Rivalda

Renowned in Budapest, Rivalda is a casual but classy place, where the food is contemporary and the service very good. *Map H3 • I, Színház utca 5–9 • 489 02 36 • Open 11:30am–11:30pm daily • Dis. access • www.rivalda.net • FFFF*

3 Gundel

A Budapest legend, Gundel has been serving fine cuisine since the mid-19th century. The food is classic Hungarian, though often with a modern twist. Men are required to wear a jacket. *Map E2 • XIV, Állatkerti út 2 • 468 40 40 • Open noon–3pm & 6:30pm–midnight • Dis. access • www.gundel.hu • FFFFF*

4 Vadrózsa Étterem

Few restaurants in Budapest are as luxurious as the Vadrózsa, situated a fair distance from the city centre. Take the tram to Margaret Bridge (Buda side) and then a bus or taxi. *Map N1 • II, Pentelei Molnár utca 15 • 326 58 17 • Open noon–4pm & 7pm–midnight daily • Dis. access • www.vadrozsa.hu • FFFFF*

5 Baraka

It is essential to book ahead for arguably Budapest's best restaurant. Head chef Norbert Biró dishes up creative cuisine and divine desserts. The service at Baraka is also excellent. *Map E2 • VI, Andrássy út 111 • 483 13 55 • Open noon–2:30pm & 7–10:30pm daily • Dis. access • www.barakarestaurant.hu • FFFFF*

6 Jazz Garden

Warm summer evenings were made for places like this one. Traditional Hungarian dishes dominate the menu, and there is jazz and blues from 9pm every night throughout the summer. *Map L5 • V, Veres Pálné utca 44/a • 266 73 64 • Open 6pm–midnight daily • FF*

7 Onyx Restaurant

Connected to the legendary Gerbeaud Cukrászda *(see p14)*, Onyx offers traditional gourmet cuisine in a warm and welcoming environment. *Map K3 • V, Vörösmarty tér 7–8 • 429 90 23 • Open noon–3pm & 6–11pm Mon–Sat • Dis. access • www.onyxrestaurant.hu • FFFFF*

Live jazz and blues at Jazz Garden

Unless otherwise stated, all restaurants are open daily and accept credit cards.

Elegant interior of Gundel

8 Búsuló Juhász Étterem
The views from this traditional restaurant on the slopes of Gellért Hill are outstanding. However, the food is average, and the Gypsy band that shuttles from table to table can either be a nuisance or a delight depending on your mood.
Map C6 • XI, Kelenhegyi út 58 • 209 16 49 • Open noon–midnight daily • Dis. access • FFFFF

9 Alabárdos Étterem
If you're looking for Hungarian food as it used to be cooked, this is the only place to come. From the goose liver terrine to the delicious chicken paprika with curd strudel, everything on the menu is authentic. Prices are high, but worth every forint. *Map G2 • I, Országház utca 2 • 356 08 51 • Open 7–11pm Mon–Fri, noon–4pm & 7–11pm Sat • Dis. access • FFFFF*

10 Kisbuda Gyöngye Étterem
A unique restaurant where the service can be terrible and the decor so cluttered that you trip on the way to your table, but the food is tremendous and the ambience outrageously *ancien regime*. Gourmets and foodies love it, as it has a chef who genuinely cares about what he's serving. *Map P1 • III, Kenyeres utca 34 • 368 64 02 • Open noon–midnight Mon–Sat • FFFF*

Top 10 Hungarian Dishes

1 Libamáj Zsírjában
Goose liver, fried in its own fat, is a Hungarian speciality and is considered a great delicacy.

2 Kolbász
Classic Hungarian sausage, which is usually very spicy.

3 Bakonyi Sertésborda
Pork chop in a creamy mushroom sauce.

4 Bélszínszelet Budapest Módra
Classic Budapest beef and paprika dish, though the beef needs to be of very high quality, which it sometimes isn't in these parts.

5 Marhapörkölt Tarhonyával
Traditional Hungarian beef goulash in a hot, paprika sauce, often accompanied by soft noodles.

6 Brassói Aprópecsenye
Pork stew, strongly seasoned with garlic and paprika and served with fried potatoes.

7 Borjúbélszín Gundel Módra
Medallions of veal in a rich mushroom sauce.

8 Erdélyi Fatányéros
Popular Transylvanian platter of grilled pork and beef, richly garnished with pickles, peppers and chips. Each portion is intended for two people.

9 Töltött Paprika
Peppers stuffed with rice and mince and served in a tomato sauce – another Transylvanian favourite.

10 Halászlé
Hungarians aren't big on fish, but this carp soup, seasoned with paprika, is popular in winter.

For a key to price categories **see pp67, 73, 79, 87, 93 or 99.**

Left **Interior of the chic Ba Bar** Right **The Columbus moored on the Danube**

Top 10 Cafés, Pubs and Bars

1 Ba Bar

Ba Bar sign

Café and lounge bar where Budapest's trendy set come to eat, drink and be seen. The lighting is superb, and the sleek wooden bar is a great place to while away the hours. ⊗ *Map E4 • VII, Huszár utca 7 • 0620 919 79 79 • Open 11:30am–midnight Sun–Thu, 11:30am–3am Fri & Sat*

2 Irish Cat Pub

One of the first Irish pubs to open in Budapest, the Irish Cat Pub remains one of the city's best. Set in a cellar opposite the Hungarian National Museum, it hosts live music three or four nights a week, and is the perfect place to relax during the summer. ⊗ *Map M5 • V, Múzeum körút 41 • 266 40 85 • Open 4pm–4am Thu–Sat*

3 Abszint

Absinthe, the enticing green drink that fuelled the imaginations of philosophers and artists alike in the mid-19th century, still survives, though not in its original form. You can enjoy the modern-day version, and more besides, at this hip but welcoming bar, café and bistro on the city's classiest avenue. Splendid contemporary art adorns the walls. ⊗ *Map M2 • VI, Andrássy út 34 • 332 49 93 • Open 11am–11:30pm daily • www.abszint.hu*

Cosy interior of the Irish Cat Pub

4 Columbus

One of Budapest's best cafés is located on a boat permanently moored on the Danube. Excellent bistro food, coffee and drinks are served all day, and the boat is popular with families who come for lunch over the weekends. The evenings often get louder as people begin to dance to live music. ⊗ *Map K4 • V, Vigadó tér, 4 Port • 266 90 13 • Open noon–midnight daily*

5 Eklektika Café

A mix of live jazz, poetry readings, art exhibitions and other eclectic events made this café a favourite with Budapest's gay-friendly crowd, not to mention the fantastic ambience. You'll always find an unpretentious group of people enjoying coffee and fine wine until late in the evening. ⊗ *Map M2 • V1, Nagymező utca 30 • 226 12 26 • Open 10am–midnight Mon–Fri, noon–midnight Sat–Sun • www.eklektika.hu*

6 Big Ben Teahàz

Situated in the old part of Pest, Big Ben Teahàz is a relaxing place to take a sightseeing

Unless otherwise stated, all cafés, pubs and bars are open daily. Pubs and bars usually remain open until about 1am.

Cosy interior of the Eklektika Café

break. They have a great selection of teas. The decor is smart but understated, though it is slightly surreal to be surrounded by pictures of London. ✆ *Map L5 • Veres Pálné utca 10 • 317 89 82 • Open 10am–10pm*

7 Passion

Occupying a prime spot on the hip Liszt Ferenc square (named after the composer Ferenc Liszt), this elegant but cosy bar and restaurant serves daily food specials. In the warmer months, comfortable cane chairs are spread out across the square and are ideal for people-watching. In winter, the warm, orange interior is equally inviting. ✆ *Map M2 • VI, Liszt Ferenc tér 10 • 268 01 99 • Open 11:30am–midnight daily*

8 Mosselen Belgian Beer Café

Only a staunch Czech nationalist would dispute the fact that Belgium produces the world's best beer. There are more than 15 varieties of beer to enjoy here, from the more famous Stella Artois and Hoegaarden to lesser-known, monk-brewed delights. Also on the menu are steaming bowls of fresh mussels, flown in daily from Belgium, and beef and lamb dishes cooked in beer. ✆ *Map C2 • XIII, Pannónia utca 14 • 452 05 35 • Open 8:30–11:30am Mon–Fri, noon–midnight daily*

9 Rigoletto

The latest sounds provide a smooth backdrop to evenings at this fashionable bar, housed in a cavernous space just north of Nyugati Station. It's the kind of place that tends to fill up early and stay full until the next morning. The crowd is trendy and drinks can be expensive, but a good time is guaranteed. ✆ *Map C2 • XIII, Visegrádi utca 9 • Open 8am–11pm daily*

10 Fregatt Pub

One of the first Western-European style pubs in town, this watering hole carries a Fregatt-class ship theme and hosts live rock and country music bands. Popular since the early 1990s and still packing them in with an excellent range of beers and whiskies. ✆ *Map L5 • V, Molnár utca 26 • 318 99 97 • Open 4pm–1am Sun–Fri, 5pm–1am Sat*

Types of Hungarian bars include traditional wine bars or cellars (borozós), *beer houses* (sörözős) *and coffee bars* (eszpresszós).

Left **Interior of the Cotton Club** Centre **Fat Mo's, a famous jazz venue** Right **Zöld Pardon**

TOP 10 Clubs

A38, aboard a ship moored on the Danube

1 A38

Budapest's top dance venue is located on a ship moored on the Danube. There are three floors to choose from – the upper deck terrace for listening to the latest mellow sounds, the lower deck-level restaurant and the concert and dance hall below. A38 is also popular for classical and rock concerts, held in the hold. *Map D6 • XI, near Petőfi Bridge in Buda, Pázmány Péter rakpart • 464 39 40 • Open 4pm–4am on programme days • www.a38.hu*

2 West Balkan

This über-hip club and concert venue relocated from Kopaszi gát by the Danube to a more central Pest site but has lost none of its cool attitude and great atmosphere. Set in a converted apartment block with windows usually thrown open, guests can sit indoors or outside in the courtyard and while away the hours listening to alternative, world and electro-dance sounds. *Map E6 • VIII, Nagytemplom utca 30 • 0620 473 36 51 • Open 6pm–5am daily*

3 Cotton Club

A genuinely good attempt to recreate a Chicago speakeasy in the heart of Budapest. You'll find a restaurant, a smoking room and a gambling room, all in the cavernous cellar that houses this place. Upstairs, there are rooms where you can spend the night in case you've had one too many brandies with your cigar. *Map M1 • VI, Jókai utca 26 • 354 08 86 • Open noon–midnight daily • www.cottonclub.hu*

4 Csiga Café

During the day, this popular pub-cum-club, by the Rákóczi tér food market, moves at a leisurely pace with gentle contemporary music. At night, the pace ups to electro, hip-hop and R'n'B. The Hungarian home cooking is good value and other options include soups, salads, sandwiches and desserts. Friendly service and warm atmosphere. *Map E5 • VIII, Vásár utca 2 • 210 08 85 • Open 11am–1am Mon–Sat, 4pm–1am Sun*

5 E-Klub

Raucous, hedonistic, rude and proud – this is the club that gives Hungarian DJs a great reputation. It is split into four areas – with a second dance floor featuring 1980s retro. The music is always the latest and hardest house around, while the crowd is the most inappropriately dressed in the city. *Map P2 • X, Népligeti út 2 • 263 16 14 • Open 10pm–5am Fri–Sat • www.e-klub.hu*

Unless otherwise stated, all clubs open daily at about 9pm in the evening and stay open until 4am.

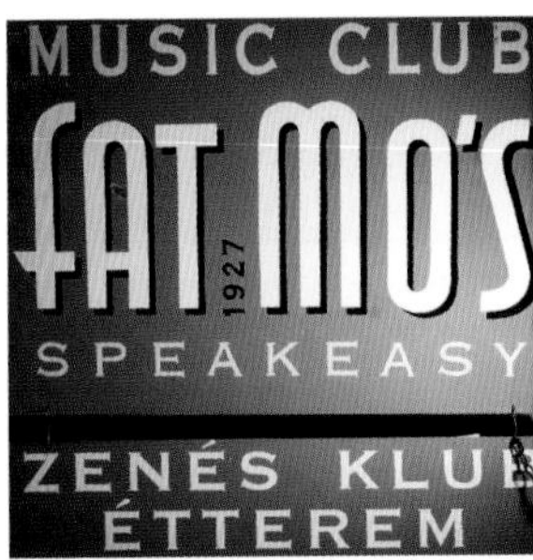

Signage for Fat Mo's speakeasy

6 Szoda

A sophisticated 24-hour café and club that only closes when they need to clean the place up. The crowd is split between well-heeled locals and in-the-know visitors, and the music is mellow – hip without being cutting edge. *Map M3 • VII, Wesselényi utca 18 • 461 00 07 • Open 9am–dawn Mon–Wed, 4pm–dawn Thu–Sun • www.szoda.com*

7 Fat Mo's

Legendary music venue that hosts regular jazz, blues and rock nights. When there are no live acts, the DJ spins the hottest dance tunes. *Map L5 • V, Nyáry Pál utca 11 • 267 31 99 • Open noon–2am Mon–Wed, noon–4am Thu–Fri, 6pm–4am Sat, 6pm–2am Sun • www.fatmo.hu*

8 Kaméleon Klub

Located on the top floor of a shopping centre, this club offers kitsch decor, kitsch music and an eclectic crowd. No matter what music is playing – usually jazz and Latino on Fridays and dance and rock on Saturdays and Sundays – you will probably have a good time, as this is one of the less pretentious clubs in town. *Map A3 • II, Mammut II Shopping Centre, 4th floor, Lövőház utca 1–5 • 345 85 47 • Open 9pm–4am Wed, Thu, Sat, 8pm–4am Fri • www.kameleonmulato.hu*

9 Zöld Pardon

This summer-only outdoor bar, concert venue and cheesy teen disco is located by Petőfi Bridge. Leave your ageist preconceptions at the gate, grab a bargain beer and listen to rock and alternative music from up and coming local bands. *Map D6 • Goldmann György tér 6 • 279 18 80 • Open Apr–Sep: 9am–6pm daily*

10 Közgáz School Club

An infamous but essential student haunt in Budapest's Corvinus University, where the drinks are cheap. Wednesday is karaoke night, and is popular. Be warned that the notoriously rude staff at the door can make getting in a hassle. *Map L6 • XI, Fővám tér 8 • 215 43 59 • Open 10pm–5am Mon–Sat*

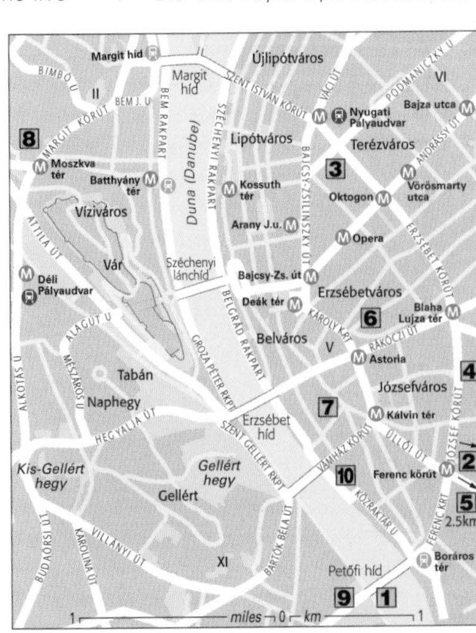

Left **Royal Palace (Grassalkovich Mansion), Gödöllő** Right **Façade of Károlyi Palace, Fót**

TOP 10 Day Trips From Budapest

1 Szentendre

A small town with cobbled lanes, pastel-coloured buildings and tall Orthodox church spires, Szentendre was originally settled in the 18th century by Serb refugees. Sights include the Hungarian Open Air Museum, which offers visitors a chance to sample country life from the 18th century until World War I, and Margit Kovács Museum, which displays the works of one of Hungary's best ceramic artists. *HÉV from Batthyány tér • Hungarian Open Air Museum: (0626) 50 25 00; open Apr–Nov: 9am–5pm Tue–Sun; adm; www.skanzen.hu • Margit Kovács Museum: (0626) 31 07 90; open 9am–5pm Tue–Sun; adm; www.szentendre.hu*

2 Gödöllő

The 18th-century Royal Palace at Gödöllő today hosts a museum and theatre. Open-air classical concerts and theatre are the highlights, but the Baroque palace and museum, especially the Palace Chapel, Franz József's salon and the gardens, are also worth a look. *HÉV from Örs Vezér tere • Royal Palace: (0628) 41 01 24; open Apr–Nov: 10am–5pm daily; Nov– Apr: 10am–5pm Tue–Sun*

3 Visegrád

The splendid ruins of a 13th-century castle are the focal point of a trip to Visegrád. It lies at the top of a hill overlooking the town below. The finest palace of its time, much of its outer wall remains. *Bus from Árpád híd • Castle: (0626) 39 80 26; Castle open May–Sep: 9am–5pm Tue–Sun; Palace open mid-Apr–mid-Oct: 9am–6pm Tue–Sun, mid-Oct–mid-Apr: 9am–4pm Tue–Sun*

Orthodox church in Szentendre's main square

4 Esztergom

This is Hungary's most sacred city as it was here that St Stephen (István) was baptized. Situated along the Danube, its main feature is a vast 19th-century cathedral. *Bus from Árpád híd; train from Nyugati pu • www.esztergom.hu*

5 Fót

Fót is home to the Károlyi Palace, the birthplace of Hungary's first president, Mihály Károlyi. The Church of the Immaculate Conception, with its columned nave, is also worth a visit. *Bus from Árpád híd; train from Nyugati pu • Palace: (0627) 35 80 23*

Emblem of the Royal Palace, Gödöllő

Fót's superb Károlyi Palace, dating from the 1830s, is open by appointment only.

6 Kecskemét

Ödön Lechner's town hall (1893–6), with pink tiles and minaret-like spires, is Kecskemét's biggest draw. Another fine building is the Secession-style Cifra Palace, built as a casino in 1902. *Train from Nyugati pu • Town Hall: (06 76) 48 07 76 • Cifra Palace: (0676) 48 07 76 • www.kecskemet.hu*

7 Kiskunfélegyháza

This town is the birthplace of the nationalist poet, Sándor Petőfi *(see p35)*, and his house is now a museum. East of town is the Kiskunfélegyháza National Park. *Train from Nyugati pu • Park: (0676) 48 26 11, tourist information: (0676) 56 14 21; open 8am–3pm*

8 Ráckeve

This town's highlight is its Orthodox church – the oldest in Hungary – which was built by Serb settlers in 1487. The interior has well-preserved frescos. *Bus from Népliget • Church: (0624) 48 59 85*

9 Martonvásár

The 19th-century Brunswick Palace at Martonvásár is one of the best preserved stately homes in Hungary. The present building is, in fact, a copy of an earlier Baroque construction, built for the Brunswick family in the late 18th century. *Train from Déli pu • Brunswick Palace: (0622) 56 95 00; open summer: 10am–noon, 2–6pm Tue–Sun; winter: 10am–noon, 2–4pm Tue–Sun • www.martonvasar.hu*

Stately mansions in the town of Vác

10 Vác

Completely destroyed and then rebuilt in the 17th century, the medieval town of Vác is best known for being the site of Hungary's Arc de Triomph built in 1764. *Train from Nyugati pu • (0627) 31 61 60 • www.tourinformvac.hu*

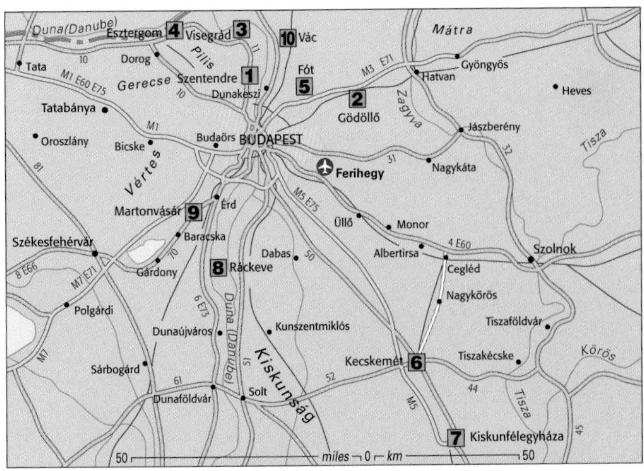

The towns featured here make ideal day trips from Budapest. Visegrád, Esztergom and Szentendre can also be reached by boat.

AROUND TOWN

Left **Budapest History Museum** Centre **Lords' Street** Right **Batthyány Square**

The Castle District and North Buda

A UNESCO WORLD HERITAGE SITE, *the medieval town of Buda grew up around a castle built by King Béla IV in the 13th century. The castle was erected on a hill that rises 170 m (558 ft) above the Danube, to protect it from invading hordes. However, it wasn't enough to repel the Turks, who ravaged and then neglected Buda in the 16th century. It was the Habsburgs who finally restored and embellished the town in the 19th century, in the glorious, Imperial style we see today. North of the castle is Víziváros (Water Town), an area first inhabited by people too poor to live on Castle Hill. Forever fighting back flood waters – the phenomenon which gives Víziváros its name – modern-day Buda, which extends as far north as the old Roman garrisons at Óbuda and Aquincum, grew out of these unlikely beginnings. Today, Víziváros is one of the most exclusive residential districts in Budapest, and home to its finest restaurants.*

Mátyás Church tower

TOP 10 Sights

1. **Royal Palace**
2. **Hungarian National Gallery**
3. **Budapest History Museum**
4. **Sándor Palace**
5. **Mátyás Church**
6. **Lords' Street**
7. **Vienna Gate Square**
8. **Church of St Mary Magdalene**
9. **Fishermen's Bastion**
10. **Batthyány Square**

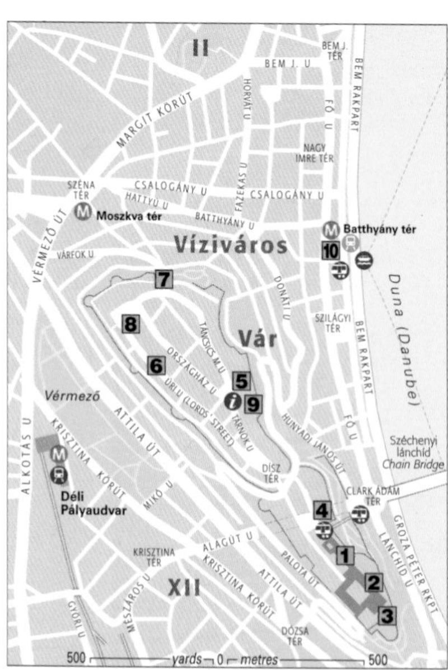

Previous pages: **Museum of Applied Arts**

The Royal Palace on Castle Hill

1 Royal Palace

Towering above Budapest, the Royal Palace, or Castle, is in fact, an amalgamation of several buildings. Most of the present Habsburg Palace was built in the 18th century during the reign of Maria Theresa, but it was preceded by a palace and two castles that had earlier stood on the site. The first castle was built around 1255, but was rebuilt by Mátyás I in 1458. Following damage in World War II, the palace was renovated again, with some parts, such as the dome, being entirely rebuilt. The last resident was Regent Admiral Horthy, who lived here from 1919 to 1945. Since then, it has housed several museums, including the Hungarian National Gallery. ⓢ *Map B4*

2 Hungarian National Gallery

It would take weeks to view all the exhibits in the National Gallery, as there are more than 40,000 works on display at any given time. From the tragedies of the 19th century to the colour and optimism of the Secession, it's all here. One of the world's greatest galleries *(see pp20–23)*.

3 Budapest History Museum

Also known as the Castle Museum, this fascinating collection of artifacts and historical documents cleverly traces the city's and the castle's history via three distinct exhibitions. The basement houses an exhibition on the castle during the Middle Ages, that includes a recreation of a vaulted chapel from the earliest 1255 structure. Gothic sculptures and armour that were unearthed while renovating the Royal Palace after World War II are also displayed. The ground floor has exhibits on the city's evolution from Roman times to the 17th century, while the first-floor exhibition is entitled "Budapest in Modern Times". ⓢ *Map J4 • I, Wing E of the Royal Palace, Szent György tér 2 • 487 88 01 • Open Mar–mid-May, mid-Sep–Oct: 10am–6pm Mon, Wed–Sun; Nov–Feb: 10am–4pm Mon, Wed–Su, mid-May–mid-Sep: 10am–6pm Mon–Sun • Dis. access • www.btm.hu • Adm*

4 Sándor Palace

This is the official residence of the Hungarian president and you can only admire the building from the outside, especially its superb Neo-Classical motifs and bas-reliefs by Richárd Török, Miklós Melocco and Tamás Körössényi. The Palace was commissioned in 1806 by Count Vincent Sándor, and designed by Mihály Pollack and Johann Aman. It was severely damaged in 1944, and was almost entirely rebuilt after World War II. ⓢ *Map H3 • I, Szent György tér 1–3 • Closed to the public*

Façade of Sándor Palace

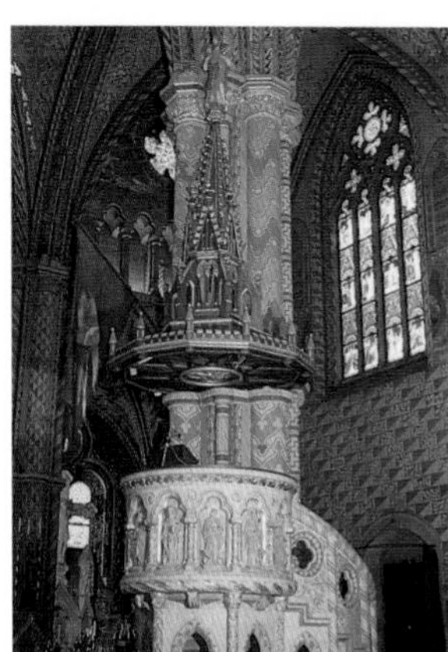

Pulpit at Mátyás Church

5 Mátyás Church

Standing on the site of a 13th-century structure, Mátyás Church was rebuilt and named after King Mátyás in 1470. Through most of the Middle Ages, Hungarians were not permitted in the church; only Germans could worship here. It has witnessed several significant events, from the marriage of Mátyás to the coronations of Franz József I and Charles IV. Béla III and his wife are also buried here. When the Turks came to power in the early 1500s, they converted Mátyás Church into a mosque. According to legend, in 1686 a statue of the Madonna appeared before the Turks while they were praying. They took this as a sign of defeat and lost the city of Buda to the Habsburgs. The church was also the scene of fierce fighting during World War II, and wasn't renovated until 1968 *(see pp24–5)*.

Alagút

The famous tunnel (alagút) that runs through Castle Hill was one of the later projects of Adam Clark, the Scottish engineer who built the Chain Bridge. Clark adored Budapest and settled here after completing the bridge. He engineered the tunnel from 1853 to 1857, and the square that faces its entrance on the Danube side bears his name. The tunnel itself, 350-m (1,150-ft) long and 11-m (36-ft) high, remains unnamed.

6 Lords' Street

Baroque and Gothic faćades give Lords' Street (Úri utca) its unique medieval character, though most of the houses were rebuilt from 1950 to 1960, after being destroyed during World War II. The street runs the full length of Castle Hill and its highlights include the Höbling House at No. 31, with its sublime Gothic façade, the Telephone Museum at No. 49, and the bizarre but exceptional Buda Castle Labyrinth *(see p45)*, whose entrance is at No. 9. The real highlight, however, is to walk from one end to the other. *Map G2; I, Úri utca*

7 Vienna Gate Square

The gate you see today is, in fact, a replica of the original structure that once led from Buda towards Vienna. It was built in 1936 to celebrate the 250th anniversary of Buda's liberation from the Turks. Quintessential Gothic and Baroque houses line the sides of the square. The huge building on the square's left-hand side is the Hungarian National Archive, a Neo-Romanesque structure famous for its multicoloured roof. *Map G1 • I, Bécsi kapu tér*

8 Church of St Mary Magdalene

Built in the 13th century for the city's Hungarian citizens, who were forbidden from praying at Mátyás Church, this church now lies in ruins. All that remains is the tower and gate, after the

The Telephone Museum (201 81 88) on Lords' Street is open 10am–4pm Tue–Sun and has an admission fee.

building was pulled down after World War II. Nevertheless, the site is enchanting, as the square in which it stands is unusually peaceful. ✎ *Map G2 • I, Kapisztrán tér 6*

9 Fishermen's Bastion

From early morning till late at night, visitors bypass Mátyás Church and head straight for the Fishermen's Bastion, whose turrets offer the most picturesque views of Pest. It was built in Neo-Romanesque style by Frigyes Schulek as a monument to the Guild of Fishermen in 1895. ✎ *Map H2 • I, Halászbástya, Szentháromság tér*

10 Batthyány Square

The heart of Víziváros, this square is named after Count Lajos Batthyány, the prime minister during the Hungarian Uprising of 1848–9. Though somewhat marred by traffic, the square retains a real charm and is crammed with architectural wonders. The Hikisch House at No. 3 has bas-reliefs depicting the four seasons, while St Anne's Church *(see p40)* is a fine Baroque building. A monument to Ferenc Kölcsey, who wrote the words of the national anthem, overlooks the Square. ✎ *Map H1 • I, Batthyány tér*

Conical tower of the Fishermen's Bastion

A Day in the Castle District & North Buda

Morning

There's no better way of getting up to the castle than by taking the **Funicular** *(see p43)* from Lánchíd utca. At the top, you can admire the stately **Sándor Palace** *(see p63)* from the outside, but you won't get past the smartly dressed guards unless you have business with the president. On the other side of the palace is the superb **Hungarian National Gallery** *(see pp20–23)*. Be careful not to stay all day; an hour or so admiring the best of Secession-period art and the collection of altarpieces on the first floor should suffice. Then stroll along the castle ramparts to **Lords' Street**, with its charming Baroque and Gothic buildings and end with a relaxing lunch at **Café Miro** (30 Lords' Street).

Afternoon

Head eastwards to the **Fishermen's Bastion** and enjoy the fabulous views of the Danube and Pest on the opposite bank; don't forget your camera. Next door is the historic **Mátyás Church** *(see pp24–5)*. You can stock up on souvenirs at any number of shops on **Fortuna utca** (the Hilton Budapest hotel, *see p112*, has a superb souvenir shop), before following the road to the ruins of the **Church of St Mary Magdalene**. From the church, take the little Castle District bus back along Lords' Street to **Ruszwurm** *(see p66)* for an elegant dinner. If you are lucky, there will be a concert at Mátyás Church to enjoy as well.

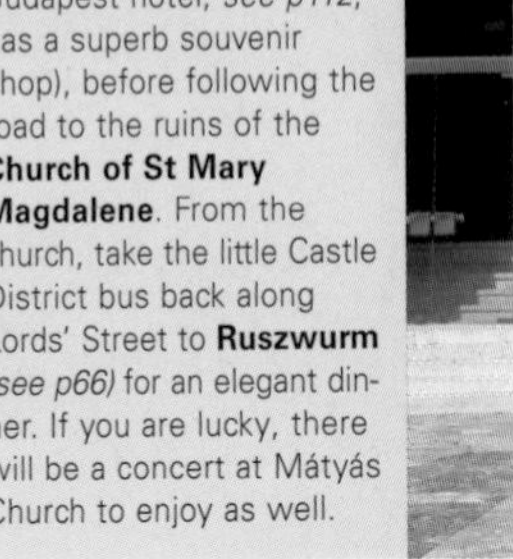

Transport in the area includes bus 16, that runs from Clark Ádám tér to Dísz tér and a minibus connecting Clark Ádám tér to Moszkva tér.

Café Gusto, located near Margaret Bridge

Top 10 Cafés, Pubs and Bars

1 Henri Belga Söröző

There are more than 20 types of Belgian beers to try at this pub, located next to a restaurant of the same name. Hoegaarden beer is a favourite. *Map J2 • I, Bem rakpart 12 • 201 50 82 • Open noon–midnight*

2 Angelika

This historic patisserie is housed in a former crypt of St Anne's Church *(see p40)*. The relaxed atmosphere and superb pastries make it popular. *Map H1 • I, Batthyány tér 7 • 212 37 84 • Open 8am–9pm daily*

3 Korona Kávéház

This excellent café is run by the same people who manage the famous Ruszwurm café. *Map H3 • I, Dísz tér 16 • 375 61 39 • Open daily*

4 Calgary Antik Drink Bar

A cross of antiques shop, bar and club, the Calgary attracts crowds long after most places have closed. *Map B2 • II, Frankel Leó utca 24 • 315 98 87 • Open 11am–4am daily*

5 Ruszwurm

Since 1824, Ruszwurm has been serving cakes and pastries to a loyal clientele. The strudel is world famous and the period furniture is worth a fortune. *Map G2 • I, Szentháromság utca 7 • 375 52 84 • Open 10am–7pm daily*

6 House of Hungarian Wines

Here you will find all the wines from Hungary's 22 wine regions. They organize daily wine tastings of up to 50 different wines. *Map G2 • I, Szentháromság tér 6 • 212 10 31 • Open noon–8pm daily • Adm*

7 Móri Borozó

Another bistro, where wine is served straight from the barrel and can be drunk by the glass. There is usually a good stew cooking as well. *Map G1 • I, Fiáth János utca 16 • 214 92 16 • Open daily*

8 Horváth

A friendly, classic pub with moderate price's and a good dinner menu. *Map G3 • I, Krisztina tér 3 • 375 75 73 • Open noon– midnight daily*

9 Oscar American Cocktail Bar

Visit this sophisticated bar to try their cocktails shaken and stirred by their great staff. *Map G1 • I, Ostrom utca 14 • 212 80 17 • Open 5pm–2am Sun–Fri, 5pm–4am Sat, 5–8pm Sun*

10 Café Gusto

Enjoy a range of salads and Hungarian food with your coffee at Gusto, located a little out of the way on the Buda side of Margaret Bridge. *Map B2 • I, Frankel Leó utca 12 • 316 39 70 • Open Mon–Sat*

Unless otherwise stated, all cafés, pubs and bars are open daily. Pubs and bars usually remain open until about 1am.

Rivalda's classic interior

Price Categories

For a three-course meal for one, with half a bottle of wine (or equivalent meal), taxes and extra charges.

F	under Ft2,500
FF	Ft2,500–5,000
FFF	Ft5,000–7,500
FFFF	Ft7,500–10,000
FFFFF	over Ft10,000

Top 10 Restaurants

1 Kacsa

You'll need a string of superlatives to describe the duck dishes at this outstanding Buda restaurant. Service is ostentatious, with dishes whipped out from under tall silver domes *(see p52)*.

2 Rivalda

Another Buda classic. The theatre-inspired decor is playful, the contemporary European cuisine superbly presented and a jazz pianist soothes the soul on most evenings *(see p52)*.

3 Alabárdos Étterem

Sensational Hungarian cuisine with a modern twist. The army of chefs make a real effort to give each dish a unique touch. Although prices are high, it is worth every forint *(see p53)*.

4 Le Jardin de Paris

This restaurant sets high standards for original French food; seafood is a speciality. It has a great terrace and garden. *Map H2 • I, Fő utca 20 • 201 00 47 • Open noon–midnight daily • FFFF*

5 Fekete Holló

This Hungarian restaurant has live Gyspy music on most evenings. The game dishes are highly recommended. *Map G2 • I, Országház utca 10 • 356 23 67 • Open 10am–10pm daily • Dis. access • FFF*

6 Budavári Fortuna Mátyás

Locals flock to this beer bar to sit at one of the long tables and drink, eat and be merry. The food is unfussy but nobody complains. *Map G2 • I, Hess András tér 4 • 375 61 75 • Open 11am–11pm daily • FF*

7 Csalogány 26

A modern restaurant serving simple Mediterranean food, most of which is charcoal-grilled on hot coals. *Map A3 • I, Csalogány utca 26 • 487 08 73 • Open 6–11pm Mon–Sat • FF*

8 Paksi Halászcsárda

Trout has never tasted so good as at this great river-fish restaurant. If you're lucky, you might catch the Gypsy band. *Map B2 • II, Margit körút 14 • 212 55 99 • Open noon–11:45pm daily • FFF*

9 Café Pierrot

This wonderful clown-themed restaurant offers great food with great service. *Map G2 • I, Fortuna utca 14 • 375 69 71 • Open 11am–midnight daily • FFF*

10 Arany Kaviar

The era of the Russian tsars is conjured up with caviar, blinis and champagne in opulent surroundings. *Map G1 • Ostrom utca 19 • 201 67 37 • Open noon–midnight daily • FFFF*

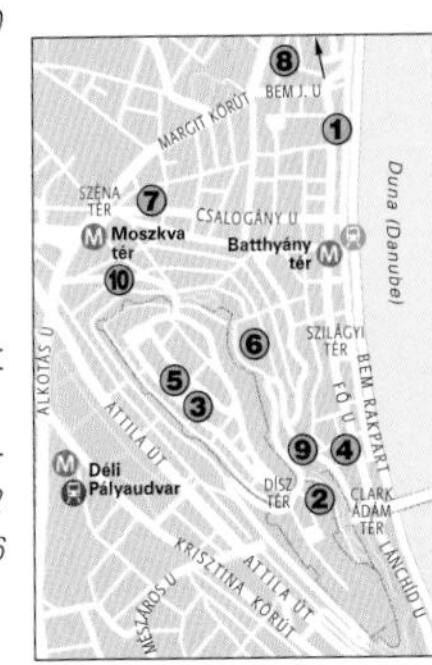

Unless otherwise stated, all restaurants are open daily – usually between 11:30am and midnight – and accept credit cards.

Left **Entrance to Cave Church** Centre **Miklós Ybl Square** Right **Bas-relief, Golden Stag House**

Gellért and Tabán

ANCIENT SUPERSTITIONS AND MEDIEVAL MYSTERIES *surround the areas of Gellért and Tabán. It is believed that Gellért Hill, which rises 140 m (460 ft) on the western bank of the Danube, was the scene of Bishop Gellért's death. In 1046, he was thrown from the top in a sealed barrel by enraged citizens, for attempting to convert them to Christianity. The hill was later the site of the Habsburgs' sinister Citadel, which even today evokes a shudder among locals. At the foot of the hill, the luxurious Gellért Hotel and Baths stand as a reminder of a gentler age. For centuries, Tabán was the city's most bohemian district, filled with numerous bars and gambling dens, until urban planners created the parks and residential areas that command some of the highest prices in the city today.*

Left **Liberation Monument** Right **Façade of the magnificent Gellért Hotel**

Top 10 Sights

1. Gellért Baths
2. Cave Church
3. Gellért Monument
4. Queen Elizabeth Monument
5. Citadel
6. Liberation Monument
7. Tabán
8. Tabán Parish Church
9. Miklós Ybl Square
10. Golden Stag House

1 Gellért Baths

Built in 1918, these are the best known and most luxurious baths in Budapest. There is a sublime main pool, with balconies, columns and stained-glass windows, as well as more traditional thermal baths. In summer, the open-air swimming pools at the back are popular with chess-playing old men who spend all day here. Although the baths are attached to the Gellért Hotel, their entrance is on the side street *(see pp16–17)*.

2 Cave Church

On Easter Monday 1951, the Hungarian secret police arrested the Pauline monks at the Cave Church, murdering the leader Ferenc Vezér and sentencing the others to long prison sentences. The church was then bricked up and forgotten until August 1989. This remarkable place of worship, which is hewn into the Gellért hillside, was founded by monks of the Pauline Order after they visited Lourdes, France, in 1926. The revived order once again presides over the church, which is closed to the public when services are in progress.
Map K6 • I, Szent Gellért rakpart 1 • 385 15 29 • Open 9am–8pm daily

Carving on the altar of the Cave Church

3 Gellért Monument

According to legend, the city's patron saint, Bishop Gellért *(see p71)* was pushed off the hill that now bears his name for attempting to convert Budapest's citizens to Christianity, including young Prince Imre, the son of Stephen I (István). Constructed in 1904, the monument to this Christian martyr is now looking a little the worse for wear, although it still retains its original majesty when viewed from afar. It is especially striking at night, when it is superbly lit. The statue and the enormous Neo-Classical colonnade that flanks it were designed by Gyula Jankovits and Imre Francsek. *Map J5*

The landmark Gellért Monument

4 Queen Elizabeth Monument

Although the wife of the Habsburg emperor, Franz József, was not Hungarian by birth, she adored her adopted subjects and made great efforts to soften Austrian attitudes towards Hungary. A number of streets, bridges and monuments throughout the nation are named after her. The monument dedicated to Elizabeth (Erzsébet) that overlooks the Danube from the Gellért embankment was designed by György Zala and erected in 1932. Its original home was on the other side of the river, from where it was removed by the Communists in 1947. It wasn't until 1986 that the statue was reinstated at its present site. *Map K5*

The ominous Citadel on Gellért Hill

5 Citadel

Built to intimidate Budapest's citizens after the failed Uprising of 1848–9, the Citadel was never actually used for its original purpose – that of quelling new revolts – as the Hungarians sought their independence by more peaceful means. Although the country was granted partial independence according to the Dual Monarchy agreement of 1867, Austrian forces occupied the Citadel until 1897. Today, it hosts a small exhibition and a restaurant *(see p73)*, and its look-out points offer great views of the city. *Map K6*

6 Liberation Monument

Perhaps the most controversial monument in Hungary, this imposing cenotaph towers above the nearby Citadel. It was originally sculpted by Zsigmond Kisfaludi Stróbl in 1943 to honour István, son of Admiral Horthy, who went missing during an air battle on the Eastern Front in 1942. However, the battle for Budapest towards the end of World War II prevented the statue's erection, and its purpose was reassigned by the Red Army in 1945 to commemorate the liberation of Budapest by Soviet forces. The inscription on the plinth originally paid tribute to the Red Army, but was changed in 1989 and now honours all those who "laid down their lives for Hungarian prosperity". *Map K6*

7 Tabán

There is little left of Tabán's original character, as its narrow streets and run-down bars on the northern slopes of Gellért Hill were cleared in 1910 to make way for scenic terraces, gardens and Secession buildings. It was one of the first areas to be inhabited in Buda – the Celtic Eravi had a settlement here from 1000 BC. The Romans later built a watchtower in the area, and in the 15th century, the Turks built the Rácz Baths *(see p37)*. In the 17th century, Tabán was home to Serb refugees, Greeks and Gypsies. Today, it is a popular venue for summer concerts, while in winter, the hillside is ideal for tobogganing. *Map H4*

8 Tabán Parish Church

This church is all that remains of Tabán's old district. Topped by a fine Neo-Baroque tower, it was built from 1728 to 1736 on the site of an earlier church that was converted to a mosque and later destroyed in the battle to overthrow the Ottoman Empire. Inside, is a copy of the 12th-century carving, *Christ of Tabán*.

Tabán Parish Church

Bishop Gellért

During a pagan revolt in the 11th century, Bishop Gellért was thrown off Old Hill in a sealed barrel. To seek forgiveness from God, the citizens of Budapest decided to dedicate the hill to him a century later. Of Italian descent, the Bishop had, in fact, been invited to Hungary to help the newly baptized St Stephen (István) spread Christianity throughout the region. It was rumoured that Stephen's brother, Prince Vata, had a hand in the martyrdom. Today, the Bishop is worshipped as Budapest's patron saint.

The original is in the Budapest History Museum *(see p63)*. The church has regular organ concerts. *Map J4 • I, Attila út 11 • 375 54 91*

9 Miklós Ybl Square

Arguably Hungary's greatest architect, responsible for gems such as St Stephen's Basilica *(see pp12–13)*, Miklós Ybl is honoured with a commemorative statue which stands in a square bearing his name. It was designed by Ede Mayer and erected here in 1894, three years after Ybl died. To the square's west are Tabán's scenic terraces, from where a number of routes lead up to the Royal Palace. *Map J4 • I, Ybl Miklós tér*

10 Golden Stag House

At the foot of Castle Hill is the Golden Stag House, named for the superb bas-relief above its entrance depicting a golden stag pursued by two hunting hounds. The 19th-century house has long been home to the Aranyszarvas restaurant. Unsurprisingly, the eatery specializes in game dishes and features venison, hare, pheasant and wild duck. *Map J4 • I, Szarvas tér 1 • 375 64 51 • Open noon–11pm daily • www.aranyszarvas.hu*

A Day in Gellért and Tabán

Morning

Start the day with a coffee and light breakfast on the corner terrace of the **Café Eszpresszó** *(see p17)* at the Gellért Hotel, then head around the corner to the **Gellért Baths** *(see pp16–17)*. Try to resist the temptation to stay all day in the various baths and swimming pools; a few hours worth of pampering and a massage should be sufficient. Once refreshed, you'll be in fine form to tackle **Gellért Hill** *(see p72)* and climb up to the **Citadel**. After enjoying the views from its ramparts, break for lunch at the Citadel's own restaurant, **Citadella** *(see p73)*.

Afternoon

After lunch, descend southwards to the **Cave Church** *(see p69)*, a bizarre place of worship hewn into the rock of Gellért Hill. From here, stroll down to Gellért Square and travel north along the embankment in the splendid tram No. 19 to **Miklós Ybl Square**. A short walk west leads you to the district of **Tabán**, where you'll be surrounded by Secession buildings. You can wander about the pretty terraces and gardens that replaced the earlier slum. Next, visit the **Tabán Parish Church** just off Attila út, one of the few surviving buildings from Tabán's old district. To the north is the fascinating **Semmelweis Museum of Medical History** *(see p72)*. End the day by enjoying a classic Hungarian meal at the Aranyszarvas restaurant in the **Golden Stag House** nearby.

Left **Exhibits at the Semmelweis Museum** Centre **Liberty Bridge** Right **Exterior of Várkert Casino**

Top 10 Best of the Rest

1 Sas Hill Nature Reserve
The reserve on Sas Hill (Sas hegy) is home to the city's strangest inhabitant, the Pannonian lizard. Access is free. *Map N2 • XI, Tájék utca 26*

2 Gellért Hill
The views from Gellért Hill, especially of the terraces below the Citadel, are among the best in the city. *Map J6*

3 Semmelweis Museum of Medical History
The house of the ground-breaking doctor Ignáz Semmelweis (1818-65) is now a museum. Exhibits include medicines from ancient Egypt to the present day. *Map J4 • I, Apród utca 1–3 • 375 35 33 • Open Mar–Nov: 10:30am–5:30pm Tue– Sun; Nov–Mar: 10:30am–3:30pm Tue–Sun • Adm • www.semmelweis.museum.hu*

4 Cistercian Church of St Imre
This Neo-Baroque church was built in 1938. Inside are relics of St Imre, patron saint of the Cistercian Order. *Map B6 • XI, Villányi út 25 • 466 44 16*

5 Technical University
Hungary's largest academic institution was built in 1904. Its alumni include Ernö Rubik, the inventor of the Rubik's Cube. *Map C6 • XI, Műegyetem rakpart 3 • 463 11 11*

6 Budapest Congress and World Trade Center
Established in 1975, this arts complex houses cinemas and conference rooms. It is best known for hosting concerts and exhibitions. *Map A5 • XII, Jagelló út 1–3 • 372 54 00 • Dis. access • www.bcc.hu*

7 Liberty Bridge
Built in 1894–9 by János Feketeházy, this bridge was originally named after Emperor Franz József *(see p43)*.

8 Former Swedish Embassy
This building was made famous by the Swedish diplomat Raoul Wallenberg, who saved tens of thousands of Jews from Nazi death camps. A monument to him stands at the corner of Szilágyi Erzsébet fasor and Nagyajtai utca. *Map K6 • XI, Minerva utca 3*

9 Várkert Casino
Budapest's most historic casino is housed in what used to be the engine room for the Royal Palace's water supply. *Map J4 • I, Ybl Miklós tér 9 • 202 42 44 • Open 11am–6am daily • www.varkert.com*

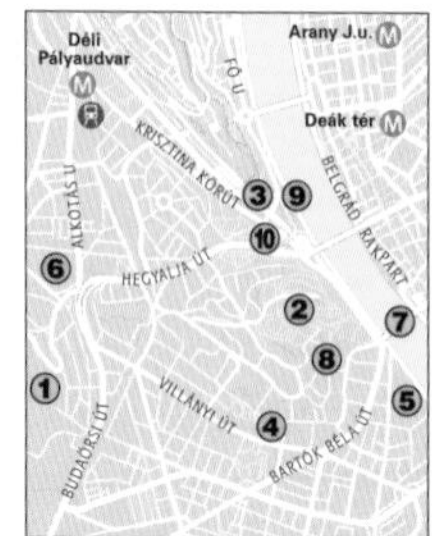

10 Rácz Baths
These ancient thermal baths, named after the Rác (Serb) population who once lived in the area, have been converted into a superb hotel spa *(see p37)*.

A guided tour to the 30-ha (75-acre) reserve on Sas Hill gives you a chance to see several extremely rare species of flora and fauna.

Exterior of Aranyszarvas

Price Categories

For a three-course meal for one, with half a bottle of wine (or equivalent meal), taxes and extra charges.

F	under Ft2,500
FF	Ft2,500–5,000
FFF	Ft5,000–7,500
FFFF	Ft7,500–10,000
FFFFF	over Ft10,000

Top 10 Restaurants, Bars and Cafés

1 Gellért Hotel

This hotel has two good restaurants – the Café Eszpressó, with its superb pastries and plaza, and the terrace restaurant, the scene of the city's best Sunday brunch *(see pp16–17)*.

2 Búsuló Juhász Étterem

The slopes of Gellért Hill provide a fabulous location for this traditional Hungarian restaurant. It specializes in game dishes and has a good wine list *(see p53)*.

3 Marcello

A somewhat spartan pizzeria serving thin and crispy pizzas at remarkably low prices. You'll need a reservation. *Map C6 • XI, Bartók Béla út 40 • 466 62 31 • No credit cards • FF*

4 Aranyszarvas

This friendly restaurant serves decently priced game specialities as well as fish and poultry. The patio opens in summer has a great view of the city. *Map J4 • Szarvas tér 1 • 375 64 51 • Open Mon–Sat (from Sep also Sun) • FF*

5 Márványmenyasszony Étterem

Quiet and secluded – until the band starts playing at 9pm – this is the perfect choice for a Hungarian meal. *Map A4 • XII, Márvány utca 6 • 487 30 90 • Open noon–midnight daily • Dis. access • FF*

6 Szeged Étterem

A Hungarian restaurant next to the Gellért Hotel. The food is good and river-fish dishes are the speciality of the house. *Map C6 • XI, Bartók Béla út 1 • 209 16 68 • Open noon–11pm daily • FFF*

7 Citadella

This restaurant's location in the Citadel's casements is much more of a draw than the food. *Map J6 • XI, Citadella sétány • 386 48 02 • Open 11am–11pm daily • FFFF*

8 János Étterem

A surprisingly good eatery in a rather nondescript hotel. The food is mainly Hungarian. *Map A5 • XI, Hegyalja út 23 • 212 91 69 • Open 7am–11am, noon–11pm • FFF*

9 Rolling Rock Pub

Great steaks and other Tex-Mex delights make this a good choice for groups of friends. You can drink late into the night and watch live acts most evenings. *Map B6 • XI, Bartók Béla út 76 • 385 33 48 • Open 11am–midnight daily • Dis. access • No credit cards • FF*

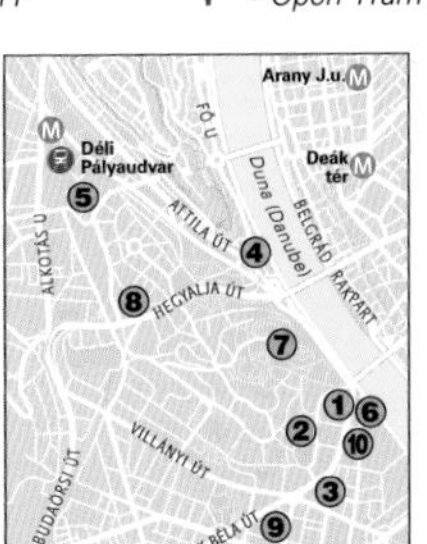

10 Kisrabló

A rough-and-ready pub and restaurant which is very popular with students. *Map C6 • XI, Zenta utca 3 • 209 15 88 • Open 11am–2am daily • Dis. access • FFF*

Unless otherwise stated, all restaurants, bars and cafés are open daily and accept credit cards. Pubs and bars remain open until about 1am.

Left **Hungarian Parliament** Right **Operetta Theatre entrance**

Around Parliament

BUDA CASTLE AND THE ROYAL PALACE *may have the benefit of their location on top of Castle Hill, but the city's defining sight remains its splendid Parliament building. The area around Parliament is redolent with history and power, with large squares, wide avenues and Secession architecture – remnants of the once powerful Austro-Hungarian Empire. The area is home to several of the city's most important buildings, including St Stephen's Basilica and the outstanding State Opera House. It also has some of Budapest's finest restaurants, as well as its most exclusive shops and residences.*

Left **Liberty Square** Right **Dome, St Stephen's Basilica**

TOP 10 Sights

1. Hungarian Parliament
2. Kossuth Lajos Square
3. Ethnographical Museum
4. Roosevelt Square
5. Academy of Sciences
6. Gresham Palace
7. St Stephen's Basilica
8. Liberty Square
9. State Opera House
10. Operetta Theatre

1 Hungarian Parliament

Constructed in 1902 to house the National Assembly, Hungary's Parliament building remains the city's primary source of civic pride. It was designed by Imre Steindl, a professor at Budapest Technical University, who won an open competition held to find an architect for the building. Inspired by London's Houses of Parliament, this magnificent edifice is filled with paintings, frescoes and tapestries by renowned Hungarian artists. The interior can only be seen by joining one of the guided tours, which take place when Parliament is not in session *(see pp8–11)*.

2 Kossuth Lajos Square

Still considered the best address in the city, Budapest's finest square is surrounded on all sides by splendid buildings. It was developed at the end of the 19th century, after the unification of Buda and Pest gave rise to large scale construction beyond the old city walls. The square is named after Lajos Kossuth, who led the 1848–9 Uprising against the Habsburgs and subsequently became a member of Hungary's first democratic government. He was exiled in 1849 after the Uprising was suppressed. A monument in front of the Parliament commemorates the Uprising. Opposite is another monument that pays tribute to Ferenc II Rákóczi, leader of the 1703 revolt against Austrian rule. A memorial to Imre Nagy, prime minister and leader of the 1956 revolt against the Soviet Union, also stands nearby. *Map K1 • V, Kossuth Lajos tér*

Sir Thomas Gresham

Although one of the city's finest buildings bears his name, Sir Thomas Gresham never set foot in Budapest. Gresham Palace *(see p76)* was commissioned over 300 years after his death by the insurance company he established. The principal figure in the founding of the London Royal Exchange, Gresham is best remembered for the maxim he made famous: "bad money drives out good".

Façade of the Ethnographical Museum

3 Ethnographical Museum

This enormous museum is housed in a splendid Neo-Classical building on the eastern side of Kossuth Lajos Square. Designed by Alajos Hauszmann, it was home to the Ministry of Justice until 1947, after which it became the Ethnographical Museum. Like the Parliament, the Museum's grand exterior and richly ornamented interior reflect the majesty of the Austro-Hungarian Empire. Although the exhibits are often overshadowed by their resplendent surroundings, the colourful displays of local costumes, toys, furnishings and wedding customs are worth a visit. *Map K1 • V, Kossuth Lajos tér 12 • 473 24 41 • Open 10am–6pm Tue–Sun • Adm • Dis. access (Szalay utca entrance) • www.neprajz.hu*

Miklós Izsó sculptures, Academy of Sciences

4 Roosevelt Square

This square has been known by various names since it was built at the head of the Chain Bridge on the Danube's eastern bank. First called Unloading Square, its name was changed to Franz József Square, to commemorate the coronation of Emperor Franz József. It was finally named after the American president Franklin D Roosevelt in 1947. Today, it features several fine hotels, including the Gresham Palace to its east. *Map K3 • V, Roosevelt tér*

5 Academy of Sciences

Inaugurated in 1864, the Academy of Sciences is a classic piece of Neo-Renaissance architecture designed by Friedrich Stüler. The statues on the façade, including those of Isaac Newton and René Descartes, are by Miklós Izsó and Emil Wolff, while the interior has more statues by Izsó. *Map J2 • V, Roosevelt tér 9 • 411 64 89 • Open 11am–4pm Mon & Fri*

Ironwork gates of Gresham Palace

6 Gresham Palace

Commissioned by the London-based Gresham Life Assurance Company and designed by Zsigmond Quittner and the brothers József and László Vágó in 1907, Gresham Palace enjoys one of Budapest's best locations opposite the Chain Bridge. It is an imposing edifice with several Secessionist characteristics, from its stained-glass windows (including one featuring a portrait of the patriot Lajos Kossuth), to the high atrium and chandelier. Today it houses a Four Seasons hotel *(see p113)*. *Map K3 • V, Roosevelt tér 5–7 • 268 60 00 • Open 8am–10pm daily (in summer organized tours are also available) • Dis. access • www.fourseasons.com*

7 St Stephen's Basilica

Visible from all over the city, the dome of St Stephen's Basilica is exactly the same height as the Parliament's own dome. The church was built on the site of Prank Theatre, where bears and wolves tore each other to shreds in front of crowds in the 18th century. Today, it is one of the city's most sacred sites, as it houses the mummified right hand of St Stephen (István), after whom the church is named *(see pp12–13)*.

8 Liberty Square

Laid out in 1886 on the site of the barracks that housed the Austrian army, Liberty Square has long been synonymous with Hungary's freedom struggle. The first prime minister of independent Hungary, Count Lajos Batthyány, was executed in

Symmetrical façade of the State Opera House

the barracks on 6 Oct 1849. The square was also the site of the 1956 protests against the Soviet Union. Today, an eternal flame at the corner of Aulich utca and Hold utca pays tribute to Lajos Batthyány, while the statue on the northern side honours the Soviet troops who liberated the city in 1944–5. *Map K2 • V, Szabadság tér*

9 State Opera House

This stunning building is one of Europe's finest concert halls, and the best way to see it is by attending a performance. World-class operas and ballets are performed almost every evening, and tickets are reasonably priced *(see pp26–7)*.

10 Operetta Theatre

Operettas (one-act or light operas) have been performed here since 1898, when the building first opened as the Orfeum Theatre. Designed by Viennese architects Fellner and Helmer, it was modified and renamed the Operetta Theatre in 1923, as it provided a home for the thriving operetta scene. It was further renovated in 1999–2001, but the interior remained faithful to the original design. *Map M2 • VI, Nagymező utca 17 • 472 20 30 • visits by appointment only • www.operettszinhaz.hu*

A Day Around Parliament

Morning

Make a mid-morning start with coffee and cakes at the café in the splendid foyer of the **Ethnographical Museum** *(see p75)*. Follow this with a leisurely stroll around the superb building, before crossing **Kossuth Lajos Square** *(see p75)* to the sensational **Hungarian Parliament** *(see pp8–11)*. Here you can join one of the guided tours, which are the only way to see the building. After this, walk along the scenic Danube embankment to **Roosevelt Square** at the head of the **Chain Bridge** *(see p42)*. You can end with a light lunch at the **Gresham Kávéház** *(see p78)* on the terrace of the **Four Seasons Hotel Gresham Palace**.

Afternoon

Walk along **Zrinyi utca**, one of Budapest's foremost residential streets, famous for its smart Secessionist-style apartment buildings, to the magnificent **St Stephen's Basilica** *(see pp12–13)* on St Stephen's Square. Climb the steps to the top of the church's dome for splendid views of the city. Then head to the **State Opera House** *(see pp26–7)*, timing your arrival to coincide with one of the daily guided tours at 3 and 4pm. Eat an early dinner at the popular **Abszint** *(see p54)* and then prepare for a night at the Opera (make sure you reserve tickets in advance). Afterwards, a drink at nearby **Picasso Point** *(see p78)* will round off a splendid day.

Left **Vadász John Bull Pub, an authentic English pub** Right **Interior, Gresham Kávéház**

TOP 10 Cafés and Pubs

1 Gresham Kávéház
The Gresham Kávéház combines elegance with a relaxed atmosphere. A range of coffees and teas as well as pastries and light meals are available. *Map K3 • V, Four Seasons Hotel Gresham Palace, Roosevelt tér 5–6 • 268 51 10 • Open daily • Dis. access*

2 Old Man's Music Pub
A great pub with live music every night of the week. It is usually packed with revellers. *Map D4 • VII, Akácfa utca 13 • 322 76 45 • Open 3pm–4am daily*

3 Európa Kávéház
This classic café is busy from morning to night with people stopping by for breakfast, a light lunch or a nightcap. *Map C2 • V, Szent István körút 7–9 • 312 23 62 • Open 9am–10pm daily • Dis. access*

4 Becketts
One of the city's best Irish pubs, Becketts serves great pub food and there's often live music on the weekends. *Map L1 • V, Bajcsy-Zsilinszky út 72 • 311 10 33 • Open daily*

5 Henry J Bean's
There's Americana everywhere in this pub. The food is good – a range of American favourites, from ribs to burgers. *Map C2 • V, Szent István körút 13 • 302 31 12 • Open noon–midnight Mon–Wed, noon–1am Thu–Sat, noon–10pm Sun*

6 Mosselen Belgian Beer Café
Belgian beer and steaming pots of fresh mussels make this a Budapest favourite. The decor is suitably sober and Belgian, but the atmosphere is lively *(see p55)*.

7 Picasso Point
The ground floor of this lively pub serves good, simple meals through the week. On the weekend the cellar turns into a disco after 11pm. *Map L2 • VI, Hajós utca 31 • 312 17 27 • Open 11am–midnight Mon–Thu, 11–4am Fri, 4pm–4am Sat, 4pm–midnight Sun*

8 Rigoletto
A bohemian cocktail bar with an extensive drinks menu. You often spot Hungarian actors relaxing here *(see p55)*.

9 Vadász John Bull Pub
An English pub serving good food and original English ale. British football is screened here on Saturday afternoons. *Map L2 • V, Podmaniczky tér 4 • 269 31 16 • Open noon–midnight daily*

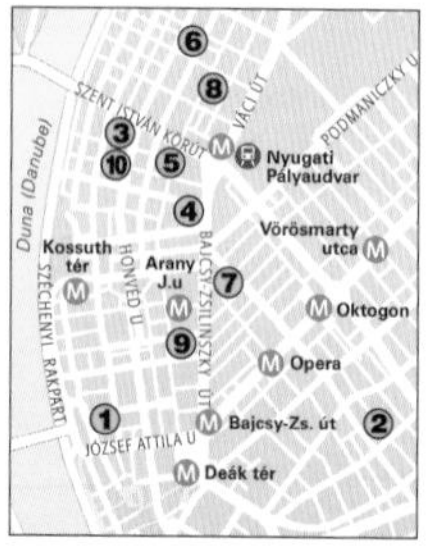

10 Tokaji Borozó
A Hungarian wine bar dedicated to sweet dessert wines from the Tokaji label. Most patrons enjoy a glass standing at the bar in traditional style. *Map C3 • V, Falk Miksa utca 30 • 269 31 43 • Open noon–9pm Mon–Fri*

Unless otherwise stated, all cafés and pubs are open daily. Pubs and bars usually remain open until about 1am.

Marquis de Salade

Price Categories

For a three-course meal for one, with half a bottle of wine (or equivalent meal), taxes and extra charges.		
	F	under Ft2,500
	FF	Ft2,500–5,000
	FFF	Ft5,000–7,500
	FFFF	Ft7,500–10,000
	FFFFF	over Ft10,000

Top 10 Restaurants

1 Abszint

Classic Provençale cuisine is served in a classy bistro setting. Abszint is a popular venue with contemporary art displayed on the walls *(see p54).*

2 Iguana

Excellent Tex-Mex fare in a lively setting. Delicious fajitas, home-made tortillas and burritos come in large portions at reasonable prices. *Map K2 • V, Zoltán utca 16 • 301 02 15 • Open daily • Dis. access • FFF*

3 Hanna

Open only at lunchtime and reminiscent of a school canteen, Hanna is a legendary Kosher eatery. A perfect choice for a good, cheap lunch. *Map M3 • VII, Dob utca 35 • 342 10 72 • Open noon–3pm Sun–Fri (Fri evening as well) • FF*

4 Admiral

The decor is inspired by the interior of an old sailing ship and there is a terrace with great views over the city. *Map K4 • V, Belgrád rakpart 30 • 318 07 23 • Open daily • FF*

5 Mare Croaticum

The fish dishes are the main attraction at this good Croatian restaurant. Other specialities include *cevap* – small, spicy meatballs. *Map L1 • VI, Nagymező utca 49 • 311 73 45 • Open noon–11pm • Dis. access • FFF*

6 Belcanto

You'll need a reservation for this classy restaurant serving inventive Hungarian cuisine. *Map L2 • VI, Dalszínház utca 8 • 269 27 86 • Open daily • Dis. access • FFFF*

7 Sir Lancelot

The city's best themed restaurant serves huge portions of medieval dishes, from marrow bones and pork knuckles to whole geese and chickens. *Map C3 • VI, Podmaniczky utca 14 • 302 44 56 • Open noon–1am • FFF*

8 Aranybárány

Right in the historical part of Pest, offering traditional Hungarian dishes. *Map K3 • V, Harmincad utca 4 • 317 27 07 • FFF*

9 Marquis de Salade

Featured in every Budapest guide book, this bistro serves a range of dishes from the countries of the former Soviet Union, especially Azerbaijan, and includes a good vegetarian selection. *Map L2 • VI, Hajós utca 43 • 302 40 86 • Open noon–1am daily • FFFF*

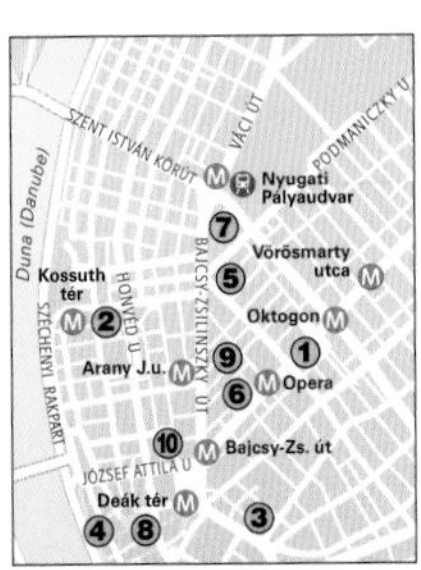

10 Café Kör

This eatery is legendary among the expat community, who flock here for the light meals, good drinks and great atmosphere. *Map L3 • V, Sas utca 17 • 311 00 53 • Open 10am–10pm Mon–Sat • No credit cards • FFF*

Unless otherwise stated, all restaurants are open daily – usually between 11:30am and midnight – and accept credit cards.

16
2

Left **Façade of the Vigadó Concert Hall** Right **Statue of poet János Arany, National Museum**

Central Pest

MOST VISITORS TO BUDAPEST *head straight for this area, known as Belváros or the Inner City. It is the city's commercial hub, and is filled with fine buildings, shops and cafés. However, the area lay in ruins at the end of the 17th century, and was only redeveloped in the 19th century when many of Pest's most important buildings were built, including the Hungarian National Museum. Today, many of the streets and squares are entirely pedestrianized, making it an ideal place for walking, shopping and dining outdoors. In fact, during the summer, the southern end of Váci utca becomes a never-ending mêlée of cafés and pubs, with revellers drinking on the pavement from dawn to dusk.*

Left **Outdoor café on Váci utca** Right **One of the Great Synagogue's twin towers**

TOP 10 Sights

1. Váci utca
2. Vigadó Square
3. Inner City Parish Church
4. Vörösmarty Square
5. Corvinus University of Budapest
6. Hungarian National Museum
7. Museum of Applied Arts
8. Great Synagogue
9. Jewish Quarter
10. Mihály Pollack Square

Previous pages: **Boats anchored on the Danube**

1 Váci utca

One of Pest's oldest streets, Váci utca originally led to the town of Vác *(see p59)*. It has long been synonymous with traders and swindlers, who clustered around Vác Gate at Váci utca 3. As Pest prospered, so did the street, and it soon became a favourite among Budapest's wealthy citizens. The goods stores gave way to exclusive boutiques, and today it is the city's most popular shopping venue. The northern half is dominated by retail outlets and department stores. The pedestrianized southern end of Váci utca is home to some of the area's best cafés and clubs *(see pp14–15)*.

2 Vigadó Square

Facing the Danube, Vigadó Square is one of Budapest's quietest spots. It is dominated by the Vigadó Concert Hall, under whose sublime colonnades visitors seek shade during hot summer afternoons. Built from 1859 to 1864 and designed by Frigyes Feszl, it replaced an earlier hall that was destroyed during the 1848–9 Uprising. The façade is a wonder of arched windows, statues and busts. Taking pride of place at the façade's centre is a Hungarian coat of arms. Badly damaged in World War II, restoration efforts have faithfully returned the building back to its former glory. Facing the Hall is the Modernist Budapest Marriott Hotel *(see p112)*, built in 1969. The jetties on the square's embankment are the departure point for Danube river cruises. *Map K4 • V, Vigadó tér*

Central Market Hall on Váci utca

3 Inner City Parish Church

Pest's oldest church has a long and troubled history. The original Roman-style structure was decimated by the Tartars, and its 14th-century replacement was converted into a mosque by the Turks. It was nearly destroyed again after World War II, when builders wanted to demolish it to make way for Elizabeth Bridge. Luckily, it survived, although the proximity of the approach road to its walls illustrates what a close call it was. *Map K4 • V, Március 15 tér 2 • 318 31 08 • Open 9am–7pm daily*

4 Vörösmarty Square

This splendid pedestrian plaza is named after the poet Mihály Vörösmarty, whose statue stands at its centre. Designed by Ede Telcs and built immaculately in Carrarra marble, the statue rallies the nation in the poet's own words: "Your homeland, Hungary, serve unwaveringly". The square's northern side is dominated by Gerbeaud Cukrászda *(see p14)*, Hungary's most famous coffee house. It is also worth visiting the quaint metro station. *Map K3 • V, Vörösmarty tér*

Baroque portal, Inner City Parish Church

Façade of the Corvinus University of Budapest

museum is the richest source of art and artifacts anywhere in the country *(see pp30–31)*.

5 Corvinus University of Budapest

A Neo-Renaissance masterpiece, this University was built between 1871 and 1874 to house the city's main customs house. Designed by Miklós Ybl, its façade facing the Danube is set on three levels – a colonnade supporting a balcony, with two rows of arched windows facing the river. The balustrade supports 10 allegorical figures sculpted by August Sommer. The building became the University of Economics in 1951, when it was named after Karl Marx; a statue of Marx remains in the atrium to this day. In 2000, it merged with the College of Public Administration and was renamed the Corvinus University of Budapest.
Map L6 • V, Fővám tér 8 • 482 50 00

6 Hungarian National Museum

The National Museum was founded in 1802, and owes its existence to Count Ferenc Széchenyi *(see p31)*, who donated his collections of books and art to the nation. The building was designed by Mihály Pollack and completed in 1845. In 1848, it was the scene of a historic event, when Sándor Petőfi recited his poem *Nemzeti Dal* (National Song) from the steps, thus igniting the Uprising of 1848–9. The event is re-enacted each year. The

7 Museum of Applied Arts

The opening of this museum was the finale of the city's 1896 Millennium Celebrations. Built to house the Hungarian State's sizeable collection of art, the Secessionist building was designed by Ödön Lechner and Gyula Pártos. Its distinctly Eastern style is seen in the façade's green domes and the glass-roofed courtyard. It features fine arts and crafts and traditional costumes. *Map D5 • IX, Üllői út 33–7 • 456 51 00 • Open 10am–6pm Tue–Sun • Dis. access • www.imm.hu*

8 Great Synagogue

The largest synagogue in Europe. Built in Byzantine style by the Viennese architect Ludwig Förster in 1854–9, it can house over 3,000 people. Since 1931 it has been home to the Jewish Museum *(see p38)*, with relics relating to the history of the city's Jews. The rear courtyard has a memorial to the Holocaust.
Map M3 • VII, Dohány utca 2 • 342 89 49 • Open Apr–Oct: 10am–5pm Mon–Thu, 10am–2pm Fri, Sun; Oct–Apr: 10am–3pm Mon–Thu, 10am–2pm Fri, Sun • Adm

Stained-glass window, Applied Arts Museum

Tony Curtis

Although Bernard Schwartz was born in New York in 1925, his parents were well known Hungarian actors who performed at many of Budapest's theatres before emigrating to America in 1923. Bernard, of course, found fame under his screen name, Tony Curtis but he never forgot his roots. He has long been a leading face in the city's international marketing campaigns.

9 Jewish Quarter

The Jewish Quarter is bordered by Károly körút, Dohány utca, Kazinczy utca and Király utca. Jews first settled in Hungary in the 13th century, in the area around Óbuda. In the 19th century, a second wave of Jews arrived and settled in this area, which was outside Pest's city walls at the time. The community thrived until 1941, when the first anti-Semetic laws were passed by Admiral Horthy's pro-Nazi dictatorship. In 1944, the area around the Great Synagogue became a ghetto from where tens of thousands of Jews were taken to death camps. Today, it is home to a small Jewish community with synagogues, shops and Kosher restaurants.

Map M3 • VII, Zsidó Negyed

10 Mihály Pollack Square

Named after the architect of several Neo-Classical buildings including the National Museum, this square is famous for its three palaces, built for Hungary's wealthiest aristocrats – Count Károlyi at No. 6, Prince Eszterházy at No. 8 and Prince Festetics at No. 10. The superb façades of the palaces (of which only the Festetics Palace is open to the public), make the square one of the most picturesque in the city.

Map D5 • V, Pollack Mihály tér

A Day in Downtown Budapest

Morning

A leisurely cup of coffee on the terrace of the Modernist **Budapest Marriott Hotel** *(see p112)* on Vigadó Square will set the tone for the day perfectly. Then walk a short distance east to **Váci utca** *(see pp14–15)*, with its superb retail stores on the northern side, including souvenir stalls, high-end fashion brands and fine Hungarian porcelain and crystal at **Goda** *(see p107)*. Next, visit Pest's oldest church, the **Inner City Parish Church** *(see p83)* just off Szabad Sajtó út, before eating a light lunch at **Cucina** in the Taverna hotel *(see p113)*.

Afternoon

After lunch, either take the metro from Ferenciek tere up to Astoria or walk ten minutes along the busy Kossuth Lajos utca to the **Great Synagogue** on Dohány utca. You can visit the splendid Byzantine-inspired synagogue and its excellent **Jewish Museum** *(see p38)* before paying your respects to the Jews killed in the Holocaust at the sobering **Holocaust Memorial** in the synagogue's rear courtyard. Then set about exploring the rest of the fascinating **Jewish Quarter**, which is known for its little gift shops and quaint book stores, as well as the far less ostentatious synagogues on Rumbach S utca and Kazinczy utca. End your day with a delicious Middle-Eastern dinner at the superb **Carmel Pince** restaurant (Kazinczy utca 31).

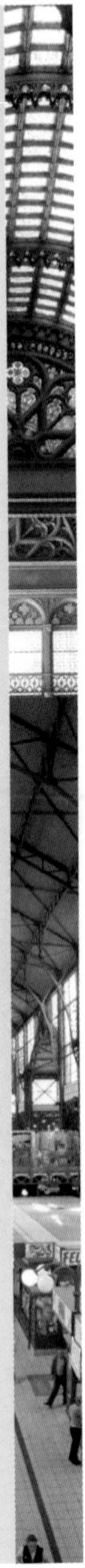

Left **Interior, Gerbeaud Cukrászda** Right **Entrance to Janis' Pub**

TOP 10 Cafés and Pubs

1 Gerbeaud Cukrászda
Beautifully decorated cakes complement the interior of the city's most famous café. Every December, there is an advent calendar window display *(see p14)*.

2 Irish Cat Pub
One of the city's best Irish pubs, the Irish Cat features good fry-ups, a friendly crowd and live music most evenings *(see p54)*.

3 1000 Tea
This café has a wide selection of teas from all over the world. With soothing music, it is the perfect place to while away long afternoons. *Map L5 • V, Váci utca 65 • 337 82 17 • Open noon–9pm Mon–Sat*

4 Cha-Cha-Cha
This student favourite has the unlikely setting of a metro station. The decor is appalling but the atmosphere second-to-none. *Map M5 • IX, Kálvin tér underpass • 215 05 45 • Open 8am–2pm Mon, Tue, 8am–3pm Wed, 8am–5pm Thu–Sat*

5 Kalamajka Dance House
If it's Hungarian folk music you want, look no further than this place. Although it caters mainly to tourists, everyone always appears to be having a great time. *Map K2 • V, Arany János utca 10 • 311 22 48 • Open 5–7pm (for children), 7pm–2am Sat*

6 Fregatt Pub
Opened in 1985, this popular pub is known for the quality blues, bluegrass and jazz bands which perform here most nights. The food is good too *(see p55)*.

7 Janis' Pub
An English-style music pub named after singer Janis Joplin. Performers entertain the crowds on most nights, and the Hungarian food is good. *Map M5 • V, Királyi Pál utca 8 • 266 26 19 • Open 4pm–2am Mon–Thu, 4pm–3am Fri, Sat, 6pm–midnight Sun*

8 Paris, Texas
A late-night favourite of the city's trendy set, who like to stop for a nightcap on their way home. The Texan link is reinforced by the malt whiskies on offer. *Map D5 • IX, Ráday utca 22 • 218 05 70 • Open 10am–3am Mon–Fri, 1pm–3am Sat & Sun*

9 Ba Bar
A chic café and lounge bar with an airy interior and superb lighting. The lounge area has white bean bags and low wooden tables *(see p54)*.

10 Mirror Café & Restaurant
An elegant café in the Hotel Astoria that manages to turn a cup of coffee into an event. *Map M4 • V, Kossuth Lajos utca 19–21 • 889 60 22 • Open 7am–11pm daily • Dis. access*

Unless otherwise stated, all cafés and pubs are open daily. Pubs and bars usually remain open until about 1am.

Smart interior of Centrál Kávéház

Price Categories

For a three-course meal for one, with half a bottle of wine (or equivalent meal), taxes and extra charges.

F	under Ft2,500
FF	Ft2,500–5,000
FFF	Ft5,000–7,500
FFFF	Ft7,500–10,000
FFFFF	over Ft10,000

Top 10 Restaurants

1 Százéves

Established in 1831, the city's oldest restaurant still serves excellent Hungarian cuisine in a fine Baroque building. *Map K4 • V, Pesti Barnabás utca 2 • 266 52 40 • FFFF*

2 Borbíróság

The "law courts of wine" venue has a legal theme and a vast array of wines on offer. *Map M6 • IX, Csarnoktér 5 • 219 09 02 • Open noon–midnight Mon–Sat • FFFF*

3 Kulacs

Visit this restaurant for its enormous portions of first-class Hungarian food and lively Gypsy band. *Map E4 • VII, Osvát utca 11 • 322 36 11 • FFF*

4 Kaltenberg Royal Bavarian Brasserie

Beer hall serving Bavarian dishes and jugs of home-brewed beer. Live accordion and sing-a-long music. Half-price meals at the weekend. *Map D5 • IX, Kinizsi utca 30–36 • 215 97 92 • Open 7am–midnight daily • FF*

5 Múzeum Kávéház és Étterem

This 1855 coffee house situated next to the National Museum serves Hungarian specialities. *Map M4 • VIII, Múzeum körút 12 • 338 42 21 • Open noon–midnight Mon–Sat • Dis. access • FFFFF*

6 Mátyás Pince

This 1904 restaurant has fine mosaics and stained-glass windows and serves exceptional Hungarian food. Live music in the evenings. *Map K4 • V, Március 15 tér 7 • 318 16 93 • FFFF*

7 Lou Lou

The food at this elegant eatery is modern French, with a twist of Hungarian. A superb wine list. *Map K2 • V, Vigyázó Ferenc utca 4 • 312 45 05 • Open noon–3pm & 7–11pm Mon–Fri, 7–11pm Sat • FFFF*

8 Mirror at Astoria

Sublime dining room in the Astoria hotel, where German forces set up camp during World War II.The food – a mix of international and Hungarian – is good. *Map M4 • V, Kossuth Lajos utca 19 • 889 60 22 • Dis. access • FFF*

9 Kárpátia

Serving classic dishes in historic surroundings, the Kárpátia is a contender for the title of Budapest's best Hungarian restaurant. *Map L4 • V, Ferenciek tere 7–8 • 317 35 96 • Dis. access • FFFF*

10 Centrál Kávéház

Standing on the site of an 1880s coffee shop, the recently restored Centrál Kávéház is a local favourite. *Map L4 • V, Károlyi Mihály utca 9 • 266 21 10 • Dis. access • FFF*

Unless otherwise stated, all restaurants and cafés are open daily – usually between 11:30am and midnight – and accept credit cards.

Left **Hungarian crest decorating the façade, Palace of Art** Right **Heroes' Square**

Around Városliget

HOME TO SOME OF THE FINEST BUILDINGS *and widest boulevards in Budapest, the area around Városliget (City Park) is where the city has long come to play. From the cafés and bistros of Liszt Ferenc tér and the mansions of Andrássy út and Városligeti fasor, to the huge City Park itself – fronted by the magnificent Millennium Monument – everything is built on a splendidly grand scale. Városliget was chosen as the centre of the city's 1896 Millennium Celebrations, and among the magnificent buildings constructed at the time were the Museum of Fine Arts and Vajdahunyad Castle.*

Left **Museum of Fine Arts** Right **Millennium Monument, dominating Heroes' Square**

TOP 10 Sights

1. Museum of Fine Arts
2. Vajdahunyad Castle
3. Széchenyi Baths
4. Andrássy Street
5. Franz Liszt Museum
6. Városligeti Avenue
7. Heroes' Square
8. Millennium Monument
9. Műcsarnok
10. Budapest Zoo

1 Museum of Fine Arts

Hungary's largest collection of international art is housed in a 1906 building designed by Fülöp Herzog and Albert Schikendanz. It has works by Raphael, Bruegel, Goya and Velazquez, as well as the largest collection of El Grecos outside Spain. *Map E2 • XIV, Hősök tere, Dózsa György út 41 • 469 71 00 • Open 10am–6pm Tue, Wed, Fri–Sun, 10am–9:30pm Thu • Dis. access • www.szepmuveszeti.hu*

2 Vajdahunyad Castle

In the middle of Városliget is the incredible Vajdahunyad Castle, a mixture of Renaissance, Gothic, Baroque and Romanesque styles, designed by Ignác Alpár for the Millennium Celebrations. Alpár's idea was to illustrate the evolution of Hungarian architecture in a single building. Each section reflects an important building and all in all the castle represents more than 20 famous Hungarian buildings. The Museum of Agriculture in the Baroque section is the only part that is open to the public. *Map F2 • Museum of Agriculture: 363 19 73; open 1 Apr–31 Oct: 10am–5pm daily; 1 Nov–31 Mar: 10am–4pm Tue–Fri, 10am–5pm Sat & Sun; Adm*

Neo-Baroque façade, Széchenyi Baths

3 Széchenyi Baths

Opened in 1913, Széchenyi is a vast complex of indoor and outpoor pools, which include Hungary's deepest and hottest thermal baths. Immensely popular in winter and summer, this is where to come if you're looking for the classic Hungarian bathing experience. *Map F2 • XIV, Állatkerti út 11 • 363 32 10 • Open May–Sep: 6am–10pm daily (some baths close at 7pm) • Adm Ft2,300 • www.budapestspas.hu*

4 Andrássy Street

A long, wide boulevard from Városliget to the city centre, Andrássy út is Budapest's most exclusive address. It is lined with fine restaurants, theatres and shops, as well as the State Opera *(see pp26–7)* and Dreschsler Palace. At No. 60 lies the former headquarters of the ÁVO, the Hungarian

View across the lake of the Gothic (left) and Renaissance (right) sections of Vajdahunyad Castle

The elegant Andrássy Street

Communist secret police who used the building from 1945 to 1956. Today, it is a museum known as the House of Terror that depicts the horrors of the Nazi and Soviet regimes. *Map L2, M2 • House of Terror: VI, Andrássy út 60; 374 26 00; open 10am–6pm Tue–Fri, 10am–7:30pm Sat & Sun; adm; www.terrorhaza.hu*

5 Franz Liszt Museum

More famously known by his Germanic name, Franz, Ferenc Liszt was Hungary's greatest composer. He lived here from 1877 until he died in 1886. The house became a museum in 1896 and the furniture, pianos and manuscripts give an insight into the life and work of this extraordinary man. *Map D3 • VI, Vörösmarty utca 35 • 322 98 04 • Open 10am–6pm Mon–Fri, 9am–5pm Sat • Adm • www.lisztmuseum.hu*

6 Városligeti Avenue

A serene tree-lined avenue, Városligeti fasor is the gentle counterpart to the more commercial Andrássy út. Numerous embassies line the avenue, and there are also several museums, including the Ráth György Museum of Far Eastern Art that houses artifacts from China and Japan brought by 19th-century Hungarian traders. There are two significant churches in the street: a Calvinist one at the southern end and a Lutheran one towards Városliget. *Map E3*

7 Heroes' Square

Communist demonstrations once took place in the vast open space of Heroes' Square. In fact, the square predates Hungary's Communist era and was originally laid out for the Millennium Celebrations of 1896. Today, people come to visit the Millennium Monument at the square's centre, while traffic runs through its southern side. It is flanked by two splendid buildings – the Museum of Fine Arts *(see p89)* and the Palace of Art. *Map E2 • Hősök tere*

8 Millennium Monument

Standing at the heart of Heroes' Square, the Millennium Monument was erected to commemorate the 1,000-year anniversary of the conquest of the Carpathian Basin by the Magyars. At the top of the 36-m (110-ft) column is a statue of the Archangel Gabriel, who allegedly offered St Stephen (István) the crown. At the foot of the column

Original furnishings in the salon, Franz Liszt Museum

The Millennium Exhibition

Much of Városliget, including the monument that marks its entrance, was built for the 1896 Millennium Exhibition, that celebrated a 1,000 years since Árpád inhabited the area near Budapest. Besides the monuments around Városliget, the exhibition saw the opening of the millennium metro line – Continental Europe's first, the installation of the city's first gas lights, and the construction of an innumerable number of Secessionist buildings.

are seven chieftains, representing the seven tribes who settled in Hungary. *Map E2 • XIV, Hősök tere*

9 Műcsarnok (Kunsthalle)

Facing the Museum of Fine Arts, the Műcsarnok (literally "market of art") was completed in 1895. The imposing building, dominated by its portico with six supporting columns, was designed by Fülöp Herzog and Albert Schikendanz. Today, it houses temporary exhibitions and concerts. *Map E2 • XIV, Hősök tere • 460 70 00 • Open 10am–6pm Tue–Sun • Dis. access • Adm • www.mucsarnok.hu*

10 Budapest Zoo

Established in 1866, the city's zoo is one of the best in Central Europe, and is known for its large primate house. There is a children's zoo where tamer animals can be petted, and various shows are held twice a day. Most of the animal houses are listed buildings, erected between 1909 and 1911 in late-Secessionist style. *Map E2 • XIV, Városliget, Állatkerti körút 6–12 • 363 37 10 • Open May–Aug: 9am–6:30pm Mon–Thu, 9am–7pm Fri–Sun; Apr & Sep: 9am–5:30pm Mon–Thu, 9am–6pm Fri–Sun; Mar & Oct: 9am–5pm Mon–Thu, 9am–5:30pm Fri–Sun • Dis. access • Adm • www.zoobudapest.hu*

A Day in City Park

Morning

Várolisget is a great place for a family outing. Start off early with a dip in Budapest's most popular thermal baths, **Széchenyi** *(see p89)*, situated right in the middle of Városliget with its own metro station on the Lilliputian Millen nium line. Refreshed, you can then take the kids next door to the **Budapest Zoo**, to admire both animals and buildings. Just north of the zoo is the park's **Funfair** *(see p45)*, with an assortment of rides. This will keep everyone happy till lunch, which can be eaten on the go from one of the funfair's numerous snack bars. Try *kolbász* – Hungarian sausages eaten by hand, that taste all the better for it.

Afternoon

Start the afternoon off at the **Museum of Fine Arts** *(see p89)* at the edge of the park in **Heroes' Square**. Although you could spend all afternoon here, try to restrict yourself to an hour and a half, but don't miss the Raphael *Madonna* or the fabulous collection of El Grecos. Then, double back to the park to the **Transport Museum** *(see p44)*, where children love climbing over old railway wagons and buses. Next, admire the architecture of **Vajdahunyad Castle**, ideally from a rowing boat on the park's central lake. If you are visiting in winter, you can take your kids ice skating on the lake *(see p44)*. Finally, end the day with a superb family dinner at **Robinson** *(see p93)*, one of Budapest's most famous restaurants.

Left **Interior of Mozart Café** Right **Exterior of the Indian café, Karma**

TOP 10 Cafés and Pubs

1 Mozart Café
The Mozart theme may be a trifle overdone (the walls are adorned with scenes from the composer's life), but the coffee is good. *Map D4 • VII, Erzsébet körút 36 • 352 06 64 • Open 9am–11pm daily*

2 Piaf
Club where the drinks are pricey, the ambience is exclusive and the decor utterly Bohemian. *Map M2 • VI, Nagymező utca 25 • 312 38 23 • Open 10pm–6am daily*

3 Barokko Club & Lounge
A restaurant, a café and a club, each on its own floor. *Map M2 • VI, Liszt Ferenc tér 5 • 322 07 00 • Open 5pm–1am Thu, 5pm–3am Fri & Sat*

4 Alhambra Art Café
Delicious Spanish and Moroccan dishes in an exotic setting. *Map M1 • VI, Jókai tér 3 • 354 10 68 • Open noon–midnight Mon–Sat, 6pm–midnight Sun*

5 Vian
Coffee, cocktails, pastas and salads make Vian a one-stop shop. Enjoy the night out on the terrace and watch the world go by. *Map M2 • VI, Liszt Ferenc tér 9 • 268 11 54 • Open 9am–1am daily*

6 Menza
Restaurant and coffee house in retro colours with a 1970s design and a modern take on Magyar canteen favourites. *Map M2 • VI, Liszt Ferenc tér 2 • 413 14 82 • Open 10am–midnight daily*

7 Incognito
Probably the most laid-back venue on Liszt Ferenc tér, this is a great place to meet people and drink cocktails. The music is strictly jazz. *Map M1 • VI, Liszt Ferenc tér 3 • 351 94 28 • Open 9am–midnight daily*

8 Karma
Superb café with Tandoori food and more cocktails than you can count. The decor is extremely Eastern. *Map M2 • VI, Liszt Ferenc tér 11 • 413 67 64 • Open 11am–2am daily*

9 Bajor Sörsátor
Hungarian beer house where drinking is taken very seriously. Wine served directly from barrels is also available. *Map F2 • XIV, Kós Károly sétány • 363 19 04*

10 Lukács Café
Legendary 19th-century café, restored to its original splendour and occupying a small corner of an international bank. *Map D3 • VI, Andrássy út 70 • 302 87 47*

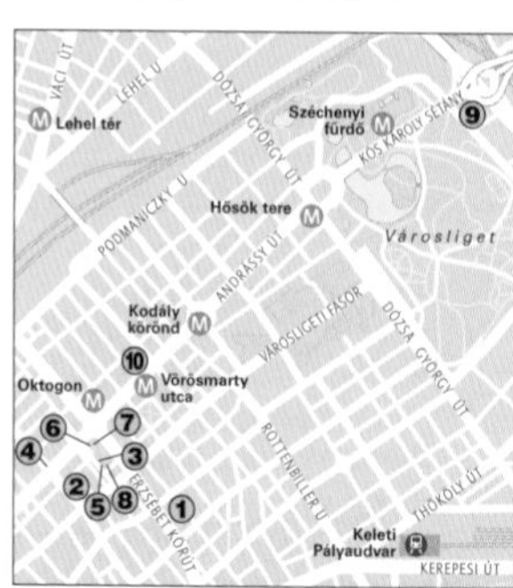

Unless otherwise stated, all cafés and pubs are open daily. Pubs and bars usually remain open until about 1am.

Price Categories

For a three-course meal for one, with half a bottle of wine (or equivalent meal), taxes and extra charges.

F	under Ft2,500
FF	Ft2,500–5,000
FFF	Ft5,000–7,500
FFFF	Ft7,500–10,000
FFFFF	over Ft10,000

Giant accordians hang from the ceiling at Hax'n Király restaurant

TOP 10 Restaurants

1 Gundel

Probably Hungary's most famous restaurant and one of the most expensive. Traditional yet adventurous food *(see p52)*.

2 Hax'n Király

This Teutonic eatery is known for sausages and wurst with sauerkraut. Lederhosen-attired men play the accordion. *Map D3 • VI, Király utca 100 • 351 67 93 • Open noon–midnight daily • FFFFF*

3 Buena Vista

Located among Liszt Ferenc tér's many bars is the Mediterranean-influenced Buena Vista. Dine indoors then head outside for drinks. *Map M2 • VI, Liszt Ferenc tér 4–5 • 344 63 03 • Open 11am–midnight daily • Dis. access • FFF*

4 Wall Street

This restaurant and bar offers seasonal specialities. Live jazz every Wednesday and Friday. *Map M2 • VI, Andrássy út 19 • 322 78 96 • Open noon–midnight • Dis. access • FFF*

5 Bagolyvár

Run by women, the Owl's Castle serves Hungarian food in a Transylvanian-style villa. *Map E2 • XIV, Állatkerti út 2 • 468 31 10 • Open noon–11pm daily • FFF*

6 Premier

Intimate restaurant with great seafood and light piano music. *Map E2 • VI, Andrássy út 101 • 342 17 68 • Open Apr–Oct: 10am–11pm Mon–Sun, Nov–Mar: 11am–11pm Mon–Sat • FFF*

7 Baraka

Budapest's best is in the Bauhaus-style MaMaison Andrássy Hotel. The menu is a delight of light, Mediterranean food and the desserts are superb *(see p52)*.

8 1894 Borvendéglő

Gundel Palace's convivial wine cellar is a great place to try local wines. The restored vaulted ceilings feature period lighting. *Map E2 • XIV, Állatkerti út 2 • 468 40 44 • Open 5–11pm Mon–Sat • Dis. access • FFFF*

9 Robinson

Set on a tiny island, Robinson is perfect if you like fresh fish and an informal ambience. *Map E2 • XIV, Városligeti-tó (City Park Lake) • 422 02 22 • Open daily • Dis. access • FFFF*

10 Maharaja

Maharaja's authentic curries, subtly flavoured with herbs and spices are delightful. *Map D3 • VII, Csengery utca 24 • 351 12 89 • Open daily • Dis. access • FFF*

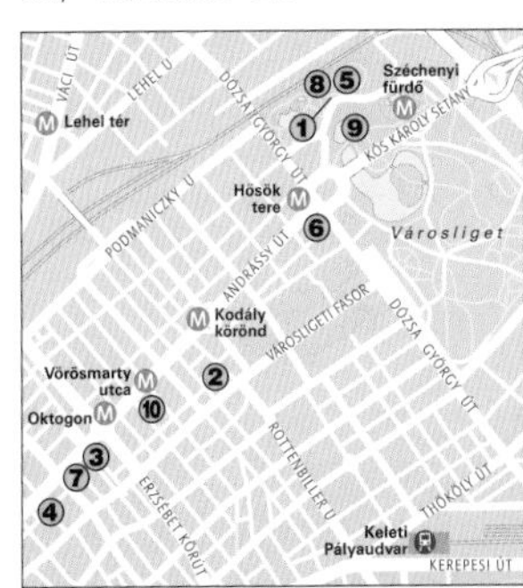

Unless otherwise stated, all restaurants are open daily between 11:30am and midnight – and accept credit cards.

Left **Public baths at Aquincum** Right **Glasshouses in the Botanical Gardens**

Greater Budapest

WHILE THE CITY CENTRE *has enough to keep most visitors happy for weeks, Budapest's suburbs have now spread out almost endlessly into the surrounding Pannonian plains and incorporate some extraordinary sights. These include the former Roman city of Aquincum, which is today bordered by a train line and a highway, as well as the former Roman garrison at Óbuda to the southwest. The Buda Hills, once some distance from the city, now have villas and apartment blocks in their foothills, while the remarkable limestone caves at Pál-völgy and Szemlő-hegy are almost lost in the city's urban sprawl.*

Top 10 Sights

1. **Buda Hills**
2. **Aquincum**
3. **Törley Mausoleum**
4. **Szemlő-hegy Caves**
5. **Pál-völgy Caves**
6. **People's Park**
7. **Geology Institute**
8. **Jewish Cemetery**
9. **Botanical Gardens**
10. **Railway History Park**

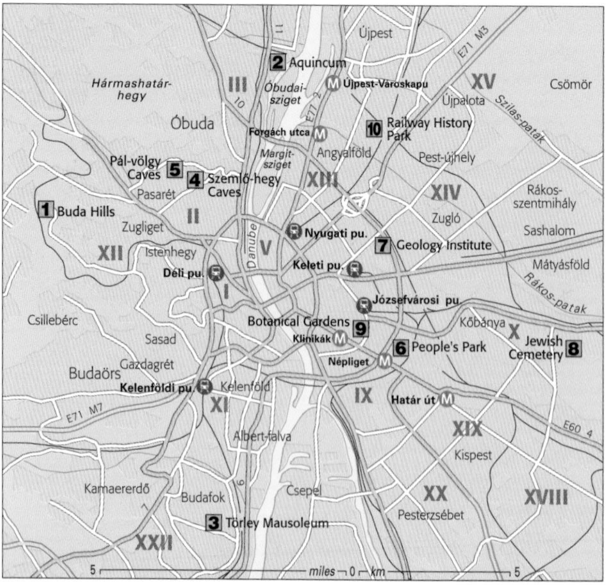

1 Buda Hills

The forested Buda Hills to the west of the city make an ideal getaway *(see p97)*. The best way to reach them is to take the Cogwheel Railway *(see p44)*, which begins at Városmajor. At the top, a short walk leads to the huge TV tower. The Children's Railway *(see p44)* begins at the base of the tower and meanders through the Buda Hills to its terminus at Hűvös Valley. En route is the Erzsébet Look-Out Tower, which has a chairlift that takes you back to Buda. It was constructed by Frigyes Schulek in 1910, but the purpose for which it was built remains a mystery. *Map N1*

2 Aquincum

The capital of the Roman province of Pannonia, Aquincum was for centuries the largest city in Central Europe. Excavated in the 19th century, it is today one of the city's most popular sights. The outlines of the streets and buildings are clearly visible. The museum, located inside a Neo-Classical Lapidarium, houses Roman artifacts found at the site, as well as models showing what the town once looked like. *Map P1 • III, Szentendrei út 139 • 250 16 50, 454 04 38 • Ruins open: Apr & Oct: 9am–5pm Tue–Sun; May–Sep: 9am–6pm Tue–Sun (museum opens 1 hour later) • Dis. access • Adm*

Central heating system, Aquincum

The Ottoman-style Törley Mausoleum

3 Törley Mausoleum

Widely recognized as the father of the Hungarian wine industry, József Törley studied the art of wine-making in Reims, France. He returned to Hungary in the 1880s, and set about producing superb sparkling wine in Budafok, a Budapest suburb. His wine sold well, making him enormously wealthy, and when he died in 1900, he was laid to rest in this mausoleum, designed by Rezső Vilmos Ray. Betraying clear Ottoman influences, it is covered in Eastern motifs and bas-reliefs and could almost be mistaken for a mosque. *Map P3 • XII, Sarló út 6*

4 Szemlő-hegy Caves

Known to many as the city of thermal waters, Budapest is also known for its caves. North of the city centre are the Pilis Hills, home to several fabulous cave systems. The Szemlő-hegy Caves are the closest to the city, on bus route No. 11 from Batthyány tér to Pusztaszeri út (it's about a mile walk from there). The caves feature splendid formations called cave pearls that look like bunches of grapes growing out of the rock. These

The dramatic Szemlő-hegy Caves

are produced when hot springs penetrate the limestone. The air here is said to be therapeutic for bronchial infections. *Map N1 • II, Pusztaszeri út 35 • 325 60 01 • Open 10am–4pm Wed–Mon • Adm*

5 Pál-völgy Caves

A hut at the foot of a steep cliff marks the entrance to the Pál-völgy Caves. As well as the cave pearl formations that are also found in Szemlő-hegy, Pál-völgy is known for its formations that are said to resemble animals. Though many of the caves are accessible, and can be visited via stairs and galleries, several of the more spectacular formations can only be seen by joining a guided tour. Note that temperatures inside the caves can be chilly. Children under five are not allowed in. *Map N1 • II, Szépvölgyi út 162 • 325 95 05 • Open 10am–4pm Tue–Sun • Adm*

6 People's Park

The city's largest park, Népliget was laid out in the 1860s and covers an area of 112 ha (277 acres). It has large tracts of grass and trees, as well as flower beds and playgrounds. It is also home to Budapest's Planetarium *(see p45)*. Népliget was also the site of the city's first motor racing track, and even hosted a Grand Prix in 1936, when Tazio Nuvolari won in his Alfa Romeo. The track fell into disuse after 1972 and when Hungary decided to host Formula One in the 1980s, a track, Hungaroring, was built outside town. *Map P2 • VIII, Népliget*

7 Geology Institute

An astonishing building opposite Hungary's National Stadium, the beautiful Geology Institute was designed by Ödön Lechner and built in 1898–9. Its roof is covered in blue Zsolnay tiles and crowned by a statue of three figures struggling to hold a globe. Inside, is a museum of rock and mineral exhibits, though Lechner's Secessionist interior is far more interesting. *Map P2 • XIV, Stefánia út 14 • 251 09 99 • Open 9am–3pm Mon–Fri • Dis. access • Adm*

8 Jewish Cemetery

Opened in 1893 and full of wonderfully elaborate tombs, this cemetery is a stark reminder of the wealth and influence wielded by Budapest's Jews before World War II. Some of the tombs were designed by leading architects, including Ödön Lechner and Gyula Fodor. *Map Q2 • XVII, Kozma út • Open 8am–2pm Sun–Fri*

The Marvellous Magyars

It may seem far-fetched, but Hungary once had the most gifted football team in the world. The legendary Ferenc Puskás led Real Madrid to three of their five European Cup triumphs after defecting to Spain. In November 1953, Hungary achieved a legendary 6–3 win over England at Wembley Stadium. The English press dubbed them the "Marvellous Magyars" and Puskás the "Galloping Major" as he was once a major in the Hungarian army.

A family day out at the Railway History Park

9 Botanical Gardens

Spread over 3 ha (8 acres) in eastern Budapest, the Botanical Gardens offer splendid relief from the bustle of the city centre. The gardens are part of Budapest University, though they were first laid out by the Festetics family, who lived in the Neo-Classical villa that is now the administration centre. They are renowned for their palm trees. *Map E6 • VIII, Illés utca 25 • 314 05 35 • Open Oct–Mar: 8am–4pm daily; May–Sep: 9am–5pm daily • Adm*

10 Railway History Park

Locomotives, luxury dining cars, passenger wagons and the Royal Hungarian Express are all on display at this open-air park, set around a few old railway sidings and sheds. You can drive an engine, ride on a railway turntable, work a hand-cart, have lunch in a dining car and then play with model trains for the rest of the day. From April to October, you can get to and from the park by taking the steam train from Keleti Station. The park also arranges steam train rides in vintage wagons to Kosice in Slovakia and Krakow in Poland. In September, it organizes a Steam Train Grand Prix, with competitors coming from all over Europe. *Map P1 • XIV, Tatai út 95 • 450 14 97 • Open Apr–early Nov: 10am–6pm Tue–Sun; Nov–mid-Dec, mid-Mar–late Mar: 10am–3pm Tue–Sun • Adm • www.mavnosztalgia.hu*

A Day in the Buda Hills

Morning

Start the day by taking bus No. 158 from Moszkva tér to its terminus at the foot of the Libegő (chair-lift), which gently takes you up to the summit of **János Hill**. From here, it is a short walk to the **Children's Railway** *(see p44)*, a splendid relic of Hungary's Communist past. As the train meanders through the hills, you can stop-off and climb to the top of the extra-ordinary **Erzsébet Look-Out Tower** *(see p95)* for sensational views of the city below. Then take the steam train which leaves on the hour throughout summer. Get off at **Szépjuhászné Station** and try the station's super outdoor café for lunch.

Afternoon

Set off on a well-marked path to the **Budakeszi Wildlife Park** (023 45 17 83; www.vadaspark-budakeszi.hu). Occupying an area of 327 ha (808 acres), it has a wide variety of animals to see, from wild boars – which also roam freely in the surrounding countryside – to packs of wolves. There is also a separate reserve for plantlife. Take the park's walking safari tour to visit its best sections. The park's own restaurant is a great place for dinner, and there is lively folk music every evening after 6pm. As the Children's Railway will almost certainly be closed by the time you finish eating, you can take bus No. 22 from outside the park straight back to Moszkva tér.

The Budakeszi Park is open Mar–Oct: 9am–4pm Mon–Fri, 9am–5pm Sat & Sun; Nov–Feb: 9am–3pm daily. It also has an admission fee.

Left **Óbuda Amphitheatre** Right **The Saxon-style Wekerle Estate**

Top 10 Best of the Rest

1 Tropicarium-Oceanarium
You can stare into the eyes of a shark or touch a snake at this aquarium and indoor tropical rainforest. *Map N3 • XXII, Nagytétényí út 37–45 • 424 30 53 • Open 10am–8pm daily • Adm • www.tropicarium.hu*

2 Óbuda Amphitheatre
Dating from around AD 140–150, this amphitheatre still has two arched entrances as well as tunnels from where wild animals entered. *Map P1 • III, Bécsi út*

3 Aquincum Amphitheatre
Once packed with 10,000 spectators, the now-ruined amphitheatre lies sandwiched between the HÉV railway and a main road. *Map P1 • III, Szentendrei út*

4 Aqueduct
A restored section of the 2nd-century aqueduct that carried water from Óbuda to Aquincum lies to the east of Szentendrei út. *Map P1 • III, Szentendrei út*

5 Flórián Square
The underpass below this square cradles Óbuda's Roman Baths and Roman Settlement Museum. *Map P1; Flórián tér • Roman Baths & Roman Settlement Museum: open 10am–5pm Tue–Sun*

6 Kassák Museum
Housed in Zichy Palace, this museum showcases the works of avant-garde artist, Lajos Kassák. *Map P1 • III, Fő tér 1 • 368 70 21 • Open 10am–6pm Tue–Sun • Adm*

7 Gizi Bajor Theatre Museum
The memorabilia at the former villa of actress Gizi Bajor honours Hungary's screen and stage stars. Exhibits include costumes, props and scripts. *Map N2 • XII, Stromfeld Aurél út 16 • 356 42 94 • Open 2–6pm Tue–Sun • Adm*

8 Nagytétény Palace
A design museum featuring classic furniture, housed in one of Hungary's best Baroque palaces. *Map N3 • XXII, Kastélypark utca 9–11 • 207 54 62 • Open 10am–6pm Tue–Sun • Adm*

9 Ludovika Academy
This former military school is now home to the Natural History Museum, where kids can touch real skulls, bones and feathers. *Map P2 • X, Ludovika tér 2–6 • 210 10 85 • Open 10am–6pm Wed–Mon • Dis. access • Adm • www.nhmus.hu*

10 Wekerle Estate
Central Europe's first Garden City, this estate was inspired by Transylvania's Saxon villages. Property here is very sought after. *Map P2 • XIX, Kós Károly tér*

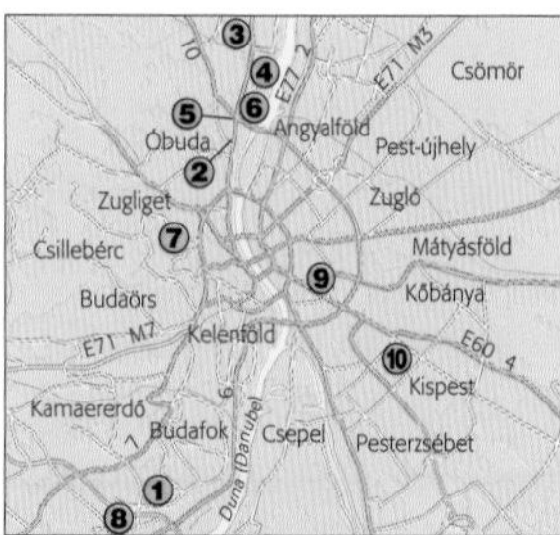

Relaxed interior of Kisbuda Gyöngye Étterem

Price Categories

For a three-course meal for one, with half a bottle of wine (or equivalent meal), taxes and extra charges.

F	under Ft2,500
FF	Ft2,500–5,000
FFF	Ft5,000–7,500
FFFF	Ft7,500–10,000
FFFFF	over Ft10,000

TOP 10 Restaurants and Cafés

1 Kisbuda Gyöngye Étterem

A lovely restaurant, with scatty decor, a lounge atmosphere and classic Hungarian cuisine served by a friendly staff. Reservations are essential *(see p53)*.

2 Kehli

Since 1899, Kehli has served old-style Hungarian food, from the period before paprika was widely used. Reservations required. *Map P1 • III, Mókus utca 22 • 250 42 41 • Open daily • Dis. access • FFF*

3 Vörös Postakocsi

Serving classic Hungarian food, the Red Mail Wagon exudes elegance despite some questionable art on its walls. For an intimate meal, ask to be seated in the library room. *Map P2 • IX, Ráday utca 15 • 217 67 56 • Open daily • FFF*

4 Chez Daniel

Excellent French cuisine, but unpredictable, eccentric service. *Map D3 • VI, Szív utca 32 • 302 40 39 • Open daily • FFF*

5 Öreghalász Étterem

A nautical-themed restaurant with a convivial atmosphere. It specializes in fish and offers five seafood soups. *Map P1 • IV, Árpád út 20 • 390 44 02 • Open daily • FF*

6 Náncsi Néni

Fantastic Hungarian eatery specializing in seasonal dishes that only use farm-fresh ingredients. *Map N1 • II, Ördögárok út 80 • 397 27 42 • Open daily • Dis. access • FF*

7 Krizia

Fresh pasta made daily on the premises, good vegetarian options and terrific desserts set Krizia apart from other Italian restaurants. *Map M1 • VI, Mozsár utca 12 • 331 87 11 • Open Mon–Sat • FFFF*

8 King Arthur's

Themed eatery in a shopping mall that shouldn't be as good as it is. The food comes in huge portions. *Map P1 • III, Bécsi út 38–44 (2nd floor, Új Udvar Shopping Centre) • 437 82 43 • Open daily • Dis. access • FFF*

9 Jardinette

Exquisite French food served around a lovely garden. The wine cellar is superb and the playground keeps the kids happy. *Map N2 • XII, Németvölgyi út 136 • 248 16 52 • Open daily • Dis. access • FFFF*

10 Taj Mahal

If the urge to go Indian grabs you, this is the only place to eat. The menu covers most Indian dishes. *Map D2 • VI, Szondi utca 40 • 301 04 47 • Open Mon–Sat • Dis. access at the corner of Rózsa utca • FFF*

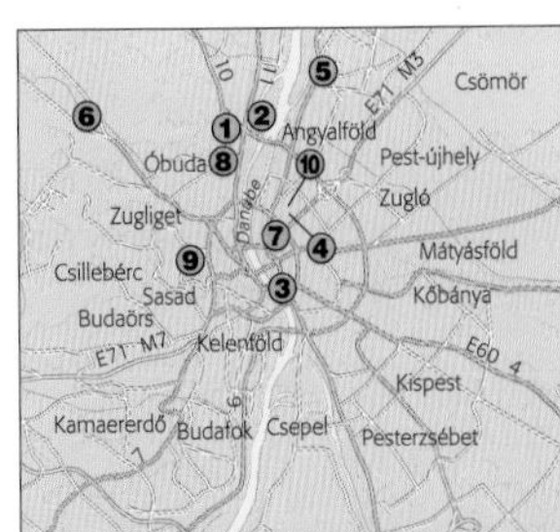

Unless otherwise stated, all eateries are open daily and accept credit cards. Restaurants are usually open between 11:30am and midnight.

STREETSMART

Left **Hungarian national airline, Malév** Centre **Tourists in Szentháromság tér** Right **Two pin plug**

Top 10 Planning Your Visit

1 When to Go

Spring and autumn are the best times to visit Budapest, as temperatures are fairly mild. Like most Central European capitals, the summer months get very busy, and finding a hotel room can be difficult. Summer can also be stiflingly hot. Christmas, however, is a delight, and almost always white, though it can get very cold.

2 Peak Seasons

The peak season is between July and August. Many locals actually leave Budapest in August for their own holidays, and the city can often feel as though it is populated entirely by tourists. Formula One weekend at the end of July is the single biggest event of the year, when hotel rooms are at their most expensive. Avoid it unless you are planning to attend the race.

3 What to Pack

Pack lightly for summer, but make sure you bring a waterproof jacket or raincoat – while temperatures are high, there are frequent, heavy showers. In winter, you will need plenty of layers to cope with the extreme climate. Hat, gloves and good footwear are also needed. If you plan on attending the opera or visiting certain top-end restaurants, men might require a jacket and tie.

4 Passports and Visas

Citizens of other European Union (EU) and European Economic Area (EEA) countries may enter Hungary without a visa and stay for as long as they please, though they should register with the local authorities after 90 days. US, Canadian, Australian, New Zealand, Bulgarian, Croatian and Romanian citizens may also enter without a visa and stay for 90 days. Citizens of almost all other countries require a visa from a Hungarian consulate before visiting.

5 Travel Insurance

Local healthcare is excellent and Hungary has reciprocal healthcare arrangements with a number of countries. However, you should still make sure that you have adequate travel insurance which includes health, trip cancellation, flight delay and lost luggage.

6 Airlines

The national airline is Malév, which flies from Budapest to over 60 destinations, including Toronto, New York and Beijing. The city is also a hub for a number of budget airlines, including Wizzair, Sky Europe, Air Berlin and easyJet.

7 Customs

If arriving from outside the EU, besides personal belongings you can bring the following items into the country – 200 cigarettes, 2 litres of wine, 1 litre of spirits and Ft350,000 worth of gifts. There are no limits on the import of goods from another EU country.

8 Electricity

The Hungarian electricity supply is 220 V and the plugs needed are the standard Continental type. Visitors from the UK and North America will need an adaptor, available at most airports.

9 Maps

There are a number of good Budapest maps available internationally, notably the Cartographia 1:20,000 series.

10 Time Zone

Hungary is in the Central European Time Zone, and is one hour ahead of Greenwich Mean Time in winter and two hours ahead in summer, six hours ahead of US Eastern Standard Time and 11 hours behind Australian Eastern Standard Time.

Directory

Malév
• *235 38 88; www.malev.com*

Budget Airlines
• *www.airberlin.de*
• *www.easyjet.com*
• *www.skyeurope.com*
• *www.wizzair.com*

Previous pages: **Lively cafés and bars in central Budapest**

Left **Train at Déli Station** Right **Luxury air-conditioned tourist coach**

TOP 10 Getting to Budapest

1 By Air
Over 40 international airlines now fly to Budapest, besides the national carrier, Malév *(see p102)*. All flights land at Ferihegy International Airport. Flights from London take around two hours, while flights from New York take about nine hours.

2 Ferihegy Airport
Ferihegy International Airport has three terminals in two locations – Ferihegy 1 is for budget airlines and is a short drive from the other terminals (linked by shuttle bus). Ferihegy 2a is for Malev, while 2b is for all other airlines. There are currency exchanges and desks for car rental companies including Avis, Hertz, Europcar and Sixt.

3 From the Airport
Ferihegy Airport lies about 16 km (10 miles) from the city centre. For around Ft2,300 the Airport Shuttle Minibus will take you anywhere in the city centre. Airport taxis *(see p104)* will take you anywhere in the city for a flat fee (Ft4,500 to the centre, Ft6,000 for the Buda side of the river) – confirm the price beforehand. There is a public bus, identified by its 200 Reptér Busz sign, to Kőbánya-Kispest metro station nearby. From Terminal 1 take bus no. 33.

4 By Train
Budapest has rail connections to more than 25 other capitals. There are three stations – one in Buda and two in Pest – and each has connections to the metro system.

5 Keleti Station
Hungary's biggest railway station is Keleti, which serves the eastern region of Hungary and is also the destination for all international trains. The station is situated approximately 3 km (2 miles) east of the city centre, on metro line M2.

6 Nyugati Station
The station closest to the city centre, Nyugati, provides train services only to the Hungarian countryside. Metro line M3 also stops here.

7 Déli Station
Trains to and from Déli Station mainly serve Lake Balaton and western Hungary. It is on metro line M2.

8 By Coach
The cheapest way to get to Budapest is by coach, and the city is served by companies all over Europe. All international coaches arrive at Népliget Bus Station in Pest, which is close to Népliget metro station on line M3.

9 By Car
Budapest is 250 km (155 miles) from Vienna, and the M1 motorway brings you to within the city limits. Since Hungary joined the EU in 2004, it has become easier to drive here, as there are now only cursory passport checks at the Austria-Hungary and Slovakia-Hungary borders. However, expect long queues at the road entry points from Croatia, Romania and the Ukraine.

10 By Boat
Arriving by boat is the most stylish way to make your entrance to the city. During summer, there are hydrofoil services from Vienna and Bratislava, which arrive at Vigadó tér *(see p42)*.

Directory

Ferihegy Airport
• *296 96 96; 296 70 00*

Train Information
• *06 40 49 49 49 (24hrs); www.elvira.hu*
• *MÁV (Hungarian Railways): 371 9449*

Coach Information
• *382 08 88 (press 3 for foreign language)*

Coach Bookings
• *www.volanbusz.hu*

Car Rentals
• *Avis: 318 41 58; www.avis.com*
• *Hertz: 296 09 97; www.hertz.hu*

Boat Services
• *Mahart Passnave: 484 4000; www.mahartpassnave.hu*

The ferry pier at Vigadó tér is just a short walk from the city centre on the Pest side of the river.

Left **Yellow city tram** Centre **Road signs for Stop and Pedestrian Zone** Right **City tour bus**

Top 10 Getting Around Budapest

1 Metro

Budapest has Europe's oldest metro system. The M1 line, with its tiny stations and three-carriage trains, opened in 1896. There are three metro lines, serving most of Pest, though little of Buda. A fourth line is in the process of being built. Trains run from 4:30am to 11:10pm. Tickets cost Ft290 or Ft260 if bought in booklets *(see p109)*. If you need to change metro lines, opt for a ticket that allows transfers.

2 Buses

Tickets can be bought from metro stations, newsstands or BKV kiosks at major stops *(see p109)*. They need to be punched in as soon as you board the bus. Buses run from 4:30am to midnight.

3 Trams

Budapest has an extensive tram network with over 30 lines. Tickets *(see p109)* need to be bought in advance. Many trams are not accessible to people in wheelchairs.

4 Taxis

Taxis are increasingly expensive. Although all have meters, you should beware using a taxi that doesn't display the name of the company it belongs to *(see p106)*. Good companies include Budataxi, Citytaxi and Főtaxi. Tariffs will be higher if you hail a taxi off the street; it is better to ring for one.

5 HÉV Trains

Budapest's suburbs, including Óbuda and Aquincum, are served by four HÉV overland trains. One line runs from Batthyány tér to Szentendre, stopping at Aquincum along the way. The second runs from Örs vezér tere to Gödöllő, taking in the Hungaroring motor racing track en route. The third runs from Közvágóhíd to Ráckeve, and the fourth from Boráros tér to Csepel Island.

6 Driving

This is the least convenient method of getting around Budapest. There are few places to park, the traffic is terrible, and the maze of one-way systems makes the city a forbidding place for uninitiated drivers. The speed limit in built-up areas is 50 km/h (30 mph), and it is forbidden to drive after consuming alcohol. Penalties for offenders are high.

7 On Foot

Perhaps the best way of getting around Budapest is on foot. Many central areas are pedestrianized, including Váci utca and the Castle District. The Danube embankment is great for walks.

8 River Boats

A number of river boat companies run services along the Danube throughout summer. Most stop at all the city's jetties on both sides of the river, as well as Margaret Island, with Vigadó tér acting as the main terminus.

9 Guided Tours

There are a number of city tours available, both on foot and by bus. Cityrama offers bus tours for around Ft7,000 per person, with departures from the Pest side of the Chain Bridge. The popular orange Hop On-Hop Off bus costs Ft5,000 and tickets last for 24 hours. For walking tours, you just need to turn up at the yellow church on Deák Ferenc tér at 9:30am or 1:30pm to meet your guide.

10 Budapest Card

The Budapest Card allows free travel on all public transport, free admission or discounts to many museums. It can be bought at the airport, stations, hotels and tourist offices *(see p109)*.

Directory

Taxi Companies
- *Budataxi: 233 33 33*
- *Citytaxi: 211 11 11*
- *Főtaxi: 222 22 22*

River Boat Tours
- *Legenda River Cruises: 317 22 03; www.legenda.hu*

Tour Companies
- *Absolute: (0630) 211 88 61; www.absolutetours.com*
- *Cityrama: 302 43 82; www.cityrama.hu*

In Budapest, seatbelts are compulsory for passengers in both the front and the back seats of cars.

Left **Façade of a tourist information office** Centre **Hungarian newspapers** Right **An Internet café**

Top 10 Useful Information

1 Tourinform

The Tourism Office of Budapest runs several Tourinform centres in Budapest. The main office is on Deák tér, and there are others at Liszt Ferenc tér, Buda Castle and the airport. They organize tours as well as offering maps and general information.

2 The Budapest Times

Available at newsstands all over the city, this weekly is the best source of local news in English. It has an excellent listings section with details of opera, cinema and sports. *The Times* also has a sister publication in German – the Budapester *Zeitung*.

3 Budacast

This excellent radio podcast is compiled by a long-term Budapest resident and fan of the city. You can listen to fascinating features on culture, music and travel, along with contributions from a wide selection of audio guests.

4 TimeOut Budapest

Monthly magazine and a welcome addition to Budapest's newsstands, *TimeOut* features articles, great photographs and superb listings on what the city has to offer, all delivered with the publication's trademark irreverent charm.

5 Visitors' Guide

Published by *The Budapest Sun* every few months, the *Visitors' Guide* provides a good overview of what's happening in the city. Given away free with the *Sun*, you should be able to find a copy at your hotel.

6 Internet

Search for Budapest on the Internet and you'll be inundated with sites – a few of the best are listed below. There are Internet cafés and wireless hotspots all over town.

7 Public Transport for the Disabled

Most buses are now accessible to the disabled, as they have entrances which can be lowered to pavement level. A few metro stations have also been made wheelchair-friendly, though trams remain inaccessible to all but the fittest, due to their steep steps.

8 Accessible Sights for the Disabled

Since Hungary joined the EU, authorities have been working to ensure that most of the country's sights are accessible to disabled visitors. However, many of the older sights are far from being wheelchair-friendly. Places that are equipped for travellers with disabilities include Mátyás Church, the Hungarian National Museum, the Parliament, the Museum of Fine Arts, St Stephen's Basilica and the State Opera House.

9 Hungarian Disabled Association

The Hungarian Disabled Association provides information on services such as transport, counselling and personal assistance. In keeping with EU regulations, all of Budapest's better hotels are equipped for disabled guests. The Association posts a list of disabled-friendly hotels on its site.

10 Gay and Lesbian Travellers

The city has innumerable gay clubs and bars, and even has exclusively gay and lesbian apartment rentals. For details, browse the excellent website which provides listings.

Directory

Tourinform
- *24-hours: 438 80 80*
- *Main office: V, Sütő utca 2, Deák tér; open 8am–8pm daily*

Tourism Websites
- *www.budapestinfo.hu*
- *www.hungarytourism.hu*
- *www.budapest.hu*

Hungarian Disabled Association
- *III. San Marco utca 76; 250 90 13; www.meosz.hu*

Gay & Lesbian Guide
- *www.budapest.gayguide.net*

The Hungarian State Tourist Office, Tourinform, also has a hotline which visitors can call from abroad: +36 30 30 30 600.

Crowds of people on Váci utca, Central Pest's main shopping street

Top 10 Things to Avoid

1 Pickpockets

Tourists are the easiest targets for petty thieves. Public transport, especially buses and metros that ferry visitors to and from the railway stations, is notorious for pickpockets. Take extra care in crowded areas such as the Castle District and Váci utca. Never carry your passport – a copy will suffice – and carry as little cash as possible.

2 Unscrupulous Taxi Drivers

Never get into a taxi that doesn't clearly state the company it belongs to, or which does not display its tariffs on the driver's door. Always ask for an estimate of the cost before getting in. Avoid taxis that lurk outside stations, as they are very expensive.

3 Keleti Station at Night

If you need to take a train from Keleti Station, note that it gets rather quiet at night. It's a favourite hang-out for slightly dodgy characters, and although crime is rare, it is an unnerving place for single travellers. It is best to wait for your train in the McDonalds or Pizza Hut across the road. Use only the main front entrance and avoid the underground walkways.

4 Girls on Váci utca

Attractive blondes on Váci utca who introduce themselves to single men may appear friendly, but alas, they are not. Refrain from joining them for a drink, even if they insist. They are "consumption girls", employed by bars to bring in foreign men to buy them drinks, which can cost as much as Ft25,000. Though many such bars were closed by the authorities, the practice continues. Check how much you're paying for a drink, and be wary of instant female friends.

5 Getting Lost

While it's unlikely you will lose your way in Budapest, note that many streets have similar names. Most famous Hungarians have squares *(tér)*, streets *(utca)* and roads *(út)* named after them. Ensure you know which one you're looking for. Many visitors confuse Váci utca, the street in the centre of town, with Váci út, the avenue north of the city centre.

6 Dog Mess

Budapest's citizens love dogs, but aren't very careful about cleaning up after them. Authorities appear to have given up on the problem, so you should watch your step.

7 Food Poisoning

Cases of lethal food poisoning are rare, but mild cases are surprisingly common, especially in less hygienic restaurants. As a rule, avoid any place that has the "tourist menu" sign outside, and be wary of eating anything cooked by street vendors.

8 Credit Card Fraud

Beware of handing over your credit card in a crowded restaurant. Some waiters have a palm-top swipe machine that can duplicate your card. Bar owners know this, and try their best to curtail the activity. When paying by card, always accompany the waiter to the cash desk. Nobody will be offended, as honest staff know why you are doing it *(see p108)*.

9 Passport "Police"

Another scam takes place while you're walking down a street. Someone stops you, and at once a "plainclothes policeman" arrests you for transacting an illegal cash deal with the man. They then ask for your passport and money, but don't hand anything over as you'll never meet a plainclothes police officer in Budapest. Walk away or shout "Police" if your way is blocked.

10 Over-Friendly Men at the Baths

Some of Budapest's baths are used by gay men to pick up partners. Single men are often approached by locals, who engage you in conversation. A polite "no thanks" will usually do the trick.

Left **Libri, a well-known bookshop** Centre & Right **Souvenirs on sale**

Top 10 Shopping Tips

1 Credit Cards

Credit cards are accepted in most places. A sign on the door usually indicates if a shop takes credit cards or not. Sometimes, however, shops refuse to accept them even when they display the requisite sign. As a norm, you will have to spend a certain minimum amount to be able to pay by credit card.

2 VAT Refunds

Non-EU residents are entitled to a VAT refund on all goods bought in Hungary, though your purchase in any one store must exceed Ft25,000. After buying what you need, ask for a Fiscal Receipt and VAT Reclaim Form, which act as export and tax refund documents. You can present these at a tax refund office at the airport or a land border, along with the goods purchased, to collect your VAT refund. A service charge of around 10 per cent is deducted when the refund amount is calculated.

3 Baskets and Bags

When entering a supermarket, make sure that you pick up a basket on entering. Failure to do so will put you under suspicion as a prospective thief. You don't receive carrier bags for your purchases as a matter of course in Budapest – they must be paid for separately.

4 Small Change

Try to keep smaller notes handy, as tellers do not like having to give you change. You will receive a rather dour look if you hand over a Ft10,000 note in a small store.

5 Specialist Shops

Although large department stores are slowly invading Hungary, Budapest is still the kind of place where small, specialist shops predominate.

6 Porcelain

There are two major manufacturers of porcelain in Hungary, Herend and Zsolnay. You will see the coloured Zsolnay tiles on many of Budapest's buildings. There is a range of porcelain shops in town, with a concentration around the northern side of Váci utca. Don't expect any bargains.

7 Crystal

Though not as famous as the Czech Republic for crystal, Budapest is still a good place to shop for it You'll find shops selling crystal on Váci utca including Goda, which has been dealing in fine Bohemian crystal for decades, and Thonet House, which sells Swarovski crystal. A famous Hungarian brand is Ajka cystal.

8 Books

Budapest must have more bookshops than any other city in Europe. For new English-language books, the best store is Bestsellers, while for second-hand books in English and Hungarian, try Red Bus Bookstore.

9 Antiques

There is no shortage of antiques shops in the city. Try the Flea Market in Városliget *(see p51)* or Ecseri Market for all sorts of rarities, Moró Antik for 18th-century weapons and BÁV for art and jewellery.

10 Souvenirs

While porcelain and antiques make great souvenirs, try the Folkart Centrum shops for handicrafts and folk costumes. It's also worth visiting Central Market Hall's *(see p50)* upper level.

Directory

Crystal
- *Goda: No 9, Váci utca; 318 46 30*
- *Thonet House: No 11, Váci utca*

Bookshops
- *Bestsellers: V, Október 6 utca 11; 312 12 95*
- *Red Bus Bookstore: V, Semmelweis utca 14; 337 74 53*

Antiques
- *BÁV: V. Bécsi utca 1; 318 44 03*
- *Moró Antik: V, Falk Miksa u. 13; 311 08 14*

Souvenirs
- *Folkart Centrum: V, Váci utca 58; 318 46 97*

For more on Budapest's shops and markets **see pp50–51.**

Left **Café Eszpresszó, Gellért Hotel** Centre **Centrál Kávéház** Right **Tea and cake at Leroy Café**

TOP 10 Eating and Drinking Tips

1 Vegetarian Tips

There are plenty of places serving vegetarian food in Budapest. Most restaurants have a vegetarian section, with dishes such as *lescó* (pan-fried tomatoes and peppers) and vegetarian goulash. Good restaurants include Krizia *(see p99)* and the Marquis de Salade *(see p79)*.

2 Ordering

When ordering meat, make sure that you clearly state how you want it cooked, otherwise it will appear the burnt side of well-done. Side dishes and vegetables are usually ordered separately. Hungarians also order their dessert along with the rest of the meal.

3 Paying

Most restaurants accept credit cards. However, some places that usually accept cards may refuse to do so if the amount spent is not considered high enough. When handing over your card to a waiter, ensure that he doesn't disappear for a while before handing it back, as he may have made a copy – a practice that is fairly common. Accompany your card to the cashier if you feel unsure *(see p106)*.

4 Tipping

Many restaurants include a service charge in the bill as a matter of course. You should feel under no obligation to pay this, as tipping is entirely at your own discretion. A 10 per cent tip for good service is usually sufficient, but if service is poor, do not feel obliged to leave any tip at all.

5 Reservations

Many of Budapest's restaurants need prior reservations, especially if you want a particular table, or would like to sit outside. You may be asked for a phone number when making a reservation – your hotel number should suffice.

6 Smoking

Hungary is increasingly unfriendly towards smokers, though you can still light up in all but the strictest bars and restaurants. Note, though, that non-smoking sections in most places are now far larger than their smoking counterparts.

7 Late-Night Eating

Unless you're willing to brave the street-stalls selling *gyros* (pita sandwiches), it can be difficult to find a midnight snack in the city. Some of the bars on Liszt Ferenc tér serve food until the early hours, and the Irish pub Becketts *(see p78)* can usually rustle up a sandwich for you as well. Remember that all central branches of McDonalds are open until midnight, while Don Pepe Pizza is open till 6am.

8 Breakfast

Even the cheapest hotel will include a Continental breakfast in the price of your room, but for something more substantial, try Chapter One for omelettes, pancakes, ham and eggs (open from 9am) or Vista, serving fresh croissants and omelettes from 8am.

9 Brunch

Sunday brunch is big news in Budapest. All the five-star hotels listed on p112 offer brunch from 11:30am, with live music, good food and often champagne for a set price, usually between Ft7,500–10,000. A favourite is at the Gellért Hotel.

10 Ethnic Food

Don't be surprised if your hot curry is not as hot as you expected. The best place for the genuine article is the Indian restaurant, Taj Mahal *(see p99)*, though Bombay Palace is also good. The city's Chinese restaurants are best avoided.

Directory

Restaurants

- *Bombay Palace: VI, Andrássy út 44; 331 19 86*
- *Chapter One: V, Nádor utca 29*
- *Don Pepe Pizza: V, Nyugati tér 8; 33 22 954*
- *Vista Café: VII, Paulay Ede utca 7; 268 08 88*

For more on Budapest restaurants, **see pp52–3, 66–7, 73, 78–9, 86–7, 92–3 and 99.**

Left **Budapest Card** Centre **Light Hungarian beers** Right **Orchestra, Academy of Music**

TOP 10 Budapest on a Budget

1 Public Transport

You will save money and time by purchasing a booklet of 10 or 20 transport tickets, or a 3 or 5-day travel pass, valid for all Budapest's bus, tram, metro and HÉV (suburban train) services, except the Buda Castle Funicular. All public transport around the city is free to EU passport holders over 65 years of age.

2 Budapest Card

Costing Ft6,300 for 48 hours and Ft7,500 for 72 hours, this card offers free travel on all public transport for the holder plus one child under 14. It allows free admission or discounts to many museums. Several restaurants offer discounts to card holders.

3 Beer

If you're looking for cheap beer, then you've come to the right place, though ensure you stick to local brews, as imported beer is expensive. Good, local brews seldom cost more than Ft300 per bottle or large glass and include Arany Ászok, Kőbányai and Dreher.

4 Food

It is still possible to eat well and cheaply, but only just. For a cheap lunch, try the Kosher restaurant Hanna *(see p79)*, or one of the Fornetti sandwich shops. Also try the falafel bar on Paulay Ede utca, where you can eat as much falafel as you can stuff into a pitta for around Ft400.

5 Accommodation

Hostels are your best option for cheap accommodation. A list of some of the best is on p117. Short-term apartments are also a good budget option *(see p116)*.

6 Student Travel

Holders of valid International Student Cards benefit from reductions on certain trains. For international travel bargains try Vista Café *(see p108)* or Wasteels in Keleti Station, both specialists in discount travel. There are no discounts for international students on public transport.

7 Museums

The entry fee for most museums, churches and other institutions is low enough to suit even the most penny-pinching visitor, and the permanent exhibitions at the big museums are usually free. However, many of these places offer discounts to students who possess a valid student ID. Note that entrance to the Hungarian Parliament *(see pp8–11)* is free for EU citizens. The thermal bath houses do not offer student discounts.

8 Opera

The State Opera House *(see pp26–7)* offers discounted tickets for seats with obscured views for as little as Ft400. Note that while your view may be limited, the sound quality is superb everywhere in the auditorium. Also, the cost of a ticket is far less than that for a guided tour – the only other way to see the inside of the building.

9 Concerts

Classical concerts are cheap, as subsidies keep prices low. The Academy of Music Liszt Ferenc is home to the Hungarian Philharmonic Orchestra, and concerts can cost as little as Ft500. The Budapest Philharmonic Orchestra, based at the State Opera House, also offers fairly cheap tickets.

10 Clubbing

Even popular clubs have free entrance on most weeknights, with only Thursday, Friday and Saturday nights commanding entry fees. In warmer months, cheap nights can be enjoyed at the open-air Zöld Pardon *(see p57)*.

Directory

Youth Hostels

- *http://budapestyouthhostel.hu*
- *www.backpackbudapest.hu*
- *www.hostels.hu*

Academy of Music Liszt Ferenc

- *VI, Liszt Ferenc tér 8; 462 46 00 or 462 46 79*

When travelling by metro, you will need to buy a new ticket each time you change lines unless you buy a ticket that allows transfers.

Left **K&H Bank logo** Centre **Local card telephone** Right **Post office sign**

TOP 10 Banking and Communications

1 Money

Hungary's currency is the forint (Ft). Coins in circulation are 1, 2, 5, 10, 20, 50, 100 and 200 Ft. Banknotes come in denominations of 500, 1,000, 2,000, 5,000, 10,000 and 20,000. It can be difficult to use Ft10,000 and 20,000 notes, especially in small stores, and is best to have smaller notes.

2 Banks

Most banks are open 9am to 5pm. Well-known banks are CIB Bank, Budapest Bank, Citibank and OTP Bank. All banks have ATM machines. They also offer the best currency exchange rates.

3 Changing Money

The best place to exchange foreign currency is in a bank. Though independent exchange houses may appear to offer better rates, they usually advertise their rates for buying, not selling, local currency, and most have hidden costs.

4 ATMs

The best way to obtain local currency is with a credit or debit card from an ATM. These are ubiquitous and though the bank that issues the card will charge a small fee for each transaction, the exchange rate is the same as that offered by the Hungarian National Bank. It is a far cheaper method than changing money or traveller's cheques.

5 Credit Cards and Traveller's Cheques

Credit and debit cards are, as a rule, universally accepted in Budapest. Traveller's cheques can usually only be changed at banks, at high commission rates. However, the American Express office cashes its own traveller's cheques free of charge.

6 Telephones

Public telephones all over the city are operated by telephone cards, available at any newsstand or post office. To find a number, call the directory service listed below. Most Hungarians have mobile phones, and the operators Vodafone, T-Mobile and Pannon offer pre-paid SIM cards at costs far cheaper than roaming charges. SIM cards are sold at most newsstands and kiosks, or you can contact local operators.

7 Post

There are post offices at both Keleti and Nyugati Stations, open from 7am to 9pm Monday to Friday (weekends vary). Apart from stamps, they offer mail-holding (poste restante) services and international phone booths.

8 Internet

There are Internet cafés at every turn in the city. Favourites are Vista Café *(see p108)* and Ami. Cafés charge upwards of Ft700 per hour.

9 Daily Newspapers

Unless you read Hungarian, you will be limited to yesterday's news, as international newspapers arrive on the following day – *The Guardian* is an exception. Foreign newspapers are available at most newsstands, but the best selection is at the World Press House.

10 Television

Although Hungarian television stations broadcast foreign programmes, all of these are dubbed into Hungarian. However, most hotels offer satellite TV, which carries international channels, including CNN, BBC and EuroNews.

Directory

Banks

- *Budapest Bank: V, Báthory utca 1; 269 41 85*
- *CIB Bank: VI, Andrássy út 70; 374 82 00*
- *Citibank: Vörösmarty tér 4; 288 23 52*
- *National Bank of Hungary: 1054 Szabadság tér 8/9; 428 26 00*

Traveller's Cheques

- *American Express: V, Deák Ferenc utca; 235 43 40*

Directory Enquiries

- *199*

Internet Cafés

- *Ami: V, Váci utca 40*

Daily Newspapers

- *World Press House: V, Városház utca 3–5*

When calling Budapest from abroad, prefix +36-1 before the local 7-digit number; within Hungary (outside Budapest), prefix 06-1.

Left **Budapest police badge** Centre **Local ambulance** Right **Interior of a pharmacy**

TOP 10 Security and Health

1 Emergency Numbers

To call an ambulance, dial 104; for police 107; for the fire service 105. Speak clearly and the operator will understand you as they all speak a variety of languages.

2 Police

If you're careful, your only brush with the city's police force is likely to be when you ask for directions. Few police officers speak English but are happy to help. The Hungarian word for police is *rendőrség*. Note that while random ID checks are rare, you are required to carry some form of identification with you at all times. A photocopy of your passport will suffice.

3 Hospitals

Budapest's hospitals are excellent, although doctors and nurses are underpaid. Do ensure that you tip them if you require their services. Most foreigners will be given free medical care in an emergency, but you should have good health insurance nevertheless. There are now many private hospitals that cater mainly to expats.

4 Fire

Don't panic in case of a fire. Tell the operator where the fire is. If you think you smell a fire in summer, it may just be smog, which descends on the city occasionally.

5 Dentists

Hungarian dental treatment is good, and cheap. If you desperately need a dentist, call SOS Dental Services or Stomatologia. Both places operate around the clock.

6 Pharmacies

The Hungarian word for pharmacy is *patika* or *gyógyszertár* although you will see the German word *apotheke* in use as well. There are many 24-hour pharmacies, though few in the centre. The closest is Déli Gyógyszertár, opposite Déli Station in Buda, and Teréz Patika, near Oktogon Metro Station in Pest.

7 Precautions

Budapest remains a very safe city, and no particular precautions are necessary, except for common sense. Avoid flashing large sums of money in public, don't get into an unmarked taxi, and do not talk to strange girls along Váci utca. Also, make sure you remember the name and address of your hotel. There is almost no violent crime in Budapest.

8 Pickpockets

Petty thieves are a fact of life in Budapest. You would do well to avoid crowded areas. Backpackers are a favourite target for pickpockets, and the buses to and from Keleti Station are their haunts *(see p106)*.

9 Food and Water Safety

Tap water is safe to drink, though given the high quality of bottled water, nobody actually does. Food poisoning is a more common problem, and the street *gyros* (pitta sandwich) stands are best avoided for this reason.

10 Consulates

Most major countries have consulates in the city. In an emergency, especially if you have any dealings with the police, insist on contacting your consulate, who will offer legal assistance.

Directory

Emergency Numbers
- *Ambulance: 104*
- *Fire Service: 105*
- *Police: 107*

Hospitals
- *Főnix S.O.S. Rt. Medical Service: 200 01 00*

Dentists
- *SOS Dental Services (24-hour): VI, Király utca 14; 267 96 02*
- *Stomatologia (24-hour): VIII, Szentkirály utca 40; 317 66 00*

Pharmacies
- *Déli Gyógyyszertár: Alkotás utca 1/B; 355 46 91* • *Teréz Patika: Teréz körút 41; 311 44 39*

Consulates
- *Canada: 392 33 60*
- *France: 374 11 00*
- *Germany: 488 35 00*
- *UK: 266 28 88*
- *USA: 475 44 00*

For more information on what to avoid in Budapest **see p106.**

Left **Lobby at the Kempinski Hotel Corvinus Budapest** Right **Façade of the Hilton Budapest**

Top 10 Luxury Hotels

1 Kempinski Hotel Corvinus Budapest

While the bold Kempinski Corvinus has a Modernist design on the outside, its inside has lush carpets, marble bathrooms and understated luxury. Most rooms overlook Erzsébet tér. *Map L3 • V, Erzsébet tér 7–8 • 429 37 77 • www.kempinski-budapest.com • FFFFF*

2 MaMaison Andrássy Boutique Hotel

At the Andrássy, you'll find all the elegance you could wish for. A member of the Small Luxury Hotels of the World group, it is situated on the city's classiest boulevard. Rooms are superbly furnished, and it has a great restaurant, Baraka *(see p93)*. *Map M2 • VI, Andrássy út 111 • 462 21 18 • www.andrassyhotel.com • FFFFF*

3 Corinthia Grand Hotel Royal

From the faithfully restored Secession façade to the exquisite atriums and foyer, the Grand Royal has been open since 1896. With its central location, lavish rooms and first class restaurants, it truly is a fabulous hotel. *Map D3 • VII, Erzsébet körút 43–9 • 479 40 00 • www.corinthiahotels.com • FFFFF*

4 Hilton Budapest

Tradition and modernity make the Hilton's façade one of the most instantly recognizable sights in the Castle District. It's a fantastic hotel, with well-furnished rooms, many of which have great views over the Danube. *Map G2 • I, Hess András tér 1–3 • 889 66 00 • www.budapest.hilton.com • FFFFF*

5 Hilton Budapest West End

Contemporary yet personal and discreet, the downtown Hilton is a celebration of space and good taste. A part of the WestEnd City Center *(see p50)*, it offers a full range of facilities as well as special services such as baby-sitters. Pets are also welcome. *Map C2 • VI, WestEnd City Center, Váci út 1–3 • 288 55 00 • www.hilton.com • FFFFF*

6 Intercontinental

Large rooms with windows overlooking the Danube are the main draw of this long-standing Budapest favourite. Common areas are welcoming, but the hotel's Corso restaurant has had mixed reviews. Business rooms come equipped with computers and Internet access. *Map K3 • V, Apáczai Csere János utca 12–14 • 327 63 33 • www.interconti.com • FFFFF*

7 Le Meridien Budapest

A perfect combination of elegance and comfort, the Meridien commands a great location on Erzsébet tér. It is a listed period piece, that has been lovingly furnished in an Art Deco style. *Map L3 • V, Erzsébet tér 9–10 • 429 55 00 • www.budapest.lemeridien.com • FFFFF*

8 Sofitel Budapest Chain Bridge

In a superb location on Roosevelt tér with views of the Danube and the Royal Palace, this hotel offers bright rooms with large bay windows. The Paris-Budapest Café, with its innovative cuisine, is a great place to relax. *Map K3 • V, Roosevelt tér 2 • 266 12 34 • www.sofitel.com • FFFFF*

9 Budapest Marriott

The first of the five-star hotels in Budapest, the Marriott dates from 1969, and its Modernist architecture still stands out on the banks of the Danube. All the rooms have stunning views. *Map K4 • V, Apáczai CsereJános utca 4 • 266 70 00 • www.marriott.com/budhu • FFFFF*

10 Radisson SAS Béke

Established in 1914, this building was entirely rebuilt in 1985. However, it retains a real charm, and is an understated treat, a place where staff have time for their guests. *Map M1 • VI, Teréz körút 43 • 889 39 00 • www.danubiushotels.com/beke • FFFFF*

All hotels in the Luxury Hotels category provide disabled access.

Entrance to the elegant art'otel

Price Categories

For a standard double room per night (with breakfast if included), taxes and extra charges.		
	F	under Ft7,500
	FF	Ft7,500–15,000
	FFF	Ft15,000–22,500
	FFFF	Ft22,500–30,000
	FFFFF	over Ft30,000

Top 10 Grand and Historic Hotels

1 Four Seasons Hotel Gresham Palace

The considerable cost of staying at the city's best hotel becomes insignificant as soon as you step into the foyer – a wonder of modern design in a classic setting. An Art Nouveau landmark, it offers splendid service and views of the Chain Bridge, Danube and the Buda Hills. *Map K3 • V, Roosevelt tér 5–6 • 268 60 00 • Dis. access • www.fourseasons.com • FFFFF*

2 Astoria

Built on the site of the medieval town walls, the Astoria is a grand, old-fashioned hotel. Its Secession exterior belies a Neo-Baroque interior, with crystal chandeliers, fine carpets and splendid works of art. *Map M4 • V, Kossuth Lajos utca 19–21 • 889 60 00 • Dis. access • No air conditioning • www.danubiushotels.com/astoria • FFFFF*

3 Danubius Hotel Gellért

Since World War I, the Gellért has been playing host to the rich and famous, who throng here to enjoy its Secession charm and thermal baths. The rooms are no longer the city's best, but are well kept and have great views over the Danube. *Map L6 • XI, Szent Gellért tér 1 • 889 55 00 • Dis. access • www.danubiushotels.com/gellert • FFFF*

4 Best Western Hotel Hungaria

Hungary's largest hotel opened in 1915, and was originally known as the Imperial. Today, it is part of the Best Western chain, and all the rooms come with superb services. *Map E4 • VII, Rákóczi út 90 • 889 44 00 • www.danubiushotels.com/grandhotel-hungaria • FFF*

5 art'otel

Situated in a sublime Neo-Baroque building on the banks of the Danube, this is a truly contemporary concept hotel, where art is a way of life. Works by American artist Donald Sultan are on display. The artistic concept incorporates everything from the carpets to the cutlery. *Map H1 • I, Bem rakpart 16–19 • 487 94 87 • Dis. access • www.artotel.hu • FFFFF*

6 Mercure Budapest City Center

Located on the city's busiest street, Váci utca, this is the perfect hotel for night-owls and shopaholics. The rooms are elegant and noise proof. *Map L4 • V, Váci utca 20 • 485 31 00 • www.mercure.com • FFFF*

7 Danubius Grand Hotel Margitsziget

Located on Margaret Island, this hotel has been entertaining Europe's aristocracy since 1873. The renovated rooms are large, with high ceilings. The hotel is connected to the adjacent Thermal Hotel by a corridor. *Map P1 • XIII, Margaret Island • 889 47 00 • Dis. access • www.danubiusgroup.com/grandhotel • FFFF*

8 Danubius Hotel Erzsébet

Named after Emperor Franz József's wife, the Erzsébet was first built in 1873, torn down in 1976, and rebuilt in 1985. Today, it is a good value hotel. Rooms are simple but large, and those on the upper floors have views of Gellért Hill. *Map L4 • V, Károlyi Mihály utca 11–15 • 889 37 00 • www.danubiushotels.com/erzsebet • FFFFF*

9 Corinthia Aquincum Hotel

A modern hotel located close to the Roman city of Aquincum. A bath complex lies adjacent, with pools and thermal baths, all free for hotel guests. *Map P1 • III, Árpád fejedelem útja 94 • 436 41 00 • Dis. access • www.corinthiahotels.com • FFFFF*

10 Danubius Health Spa Resort Margitsziget

This hotel has its own thermal bath complex, and the spa offers a range of treatments. Rooms are huge, and there are good restaurants. *Map P1 • XIII, Margaret Island • 889 47 00 • Dis. access • www.danubiushotels.com/thermalhotel • FFFFF*

Unless otherwise stated, all hotels accept credit cards, and have private bathrooms and air conditioning.

Left **Interior of the legendary Cotton House** Right **Sign for the Buda Gold hotel**

TOP 10 Mid-Range Hotels

1 K+K Hotel Opera

Part of the K+K chain, this is a classy hotel near the State Opera House, with an elegant façade and modern interiors. Rooms are well furnished, with plenty of natural light. There's a lively bar and secure car parking. *Map L2 • VI, Révay utca 24 • 269 02 22 • www.kkhotels.com • FFFF*

2 Cotton House

Upstairs at the legendary Cotton Club *(see p56)* is the Cotton House hotel, where 22 double rooms are individually named and decorated in tribute to great performers. Names as diverse as Frank Sinatra, Charlie Chaplin, Tom Jones and Ella Fitzgerald are among those honoured. *Map M1 • VI, Jókai utca 26 • 354 26 00 • www.cottonhouse.hu • FFFF*

3 Ibis Centrum

Part of the Ibis chain, where function wins over style, but high standards are guaranteed. Though located on one of the city's busiest streets, the rooms are soundproofed from the noise below. There is also a lovely garden patio. *Map M5 • IX, Ráday utca 6 • 456 41 00 • Dis. access • www.ibis-centrum.hu • FFF*

4 Hotel Victoria

Located beneath Buda Castle on the Danube embankment, this charming, mid-range hotel offers 27 spacious, well equipped rooms, all with fantastic river views. The staff are knowledgeable and helpful, and free Wi-Fi is available. *Map H2 • I, Bem rackpart 11 • 457 80 80 • www.victoria.hu • FFFF*

5 Hotel Molnár

A good hotel in the Buda Hills, set in two separate buildings – one light green, the other beige. The rooms and service are excellent in both, but the views are slightly better from the green building. *Map N2 • XII, Fodor utca 143 • 395 18 73 • www.hotel-molnar.hu • FFF*

6 Carlton Hotel

The austere-looking Carlton is, in fact, a good mid-range hotel, where all 95 rather basic but comfortable rooms have air conditioning. An excellent buffet breakfast is included in the price of your room. *Map H3 • I, Apor Péter utca 3 • 224 09 99 • www.carltonhotel.hu • FFFF*

7 Burg Hotel

The large, tastefully furnished rooms directly opposite Mátyás Church on Castle Hill, make this a popular hotel, where you need to reserve a room long before your visit. There is no better place to stay if you plan on being the first to reach Fishermen's Bastion – across the road – with your camera. *Map G2 • I, Szentháromság tér 7–8 • 212 02 69 • www.burghotelbudapest.com • FFFF*

8 Buda Gold

A splendid Buda hotel, located a short walk from the Citadella. Housed in a great building, complete with a tower, it was only built in 1997. Rooms have cherry wood parquet floors, and most have great views over the Danube or the Buda Hills. The tower rooms, which cost extra, are the best. *Map A5 • I, Hegyalja út 14 • 209 47 75 • Dis. access • www.goldhotel.hu • FFFF*

9 City Hotel Mátyás

Just a couple of minutes from Váci utca, the striking City Hotel Mátyás is located above the Mátyás Cellar, a well-known Hungarian restaurant. Rooms are comfortable and some have air conditioning. *Map K4 • V, Március 15 tér 7–8 • 338 47 11 • www.taverna.hu/matyas • FFF*

10 City Hotel Pilvax

Well hidden behind Váci utca, this is a three-star hotel in the heart of Budapest. Rooms are spartan, but comfortable and prices include a great buffet breakfast. It's tough to find better value so close to the city centre. *Map L4 • V, Pilvax köz 72 • 266 76 60 • www.taverna.hu/pilvax • FFF*

Unless otherwise stated, all hotels accept credit cards, and have private bathrooms and air conditioning.

The Boat Hotel Fortuna

Price Categories

For a standard double room per night (with breakfast if included), taxes and extra charges.

F	under Ft7,500
FF	Ft7,500–15,000
FFF	Ft15,000–22,500
FFFF	Ft22,500–30,000
FFFFF	over Ft30,000

Top 10 Small Hotels and Pensions

1 Boat Hotel Fortuna

For something different, try this hotel on the Danube, near Margaret Bridge in Pest. Some rooms are large, but some are smaller than a cabin boy's quarters. There's a restaurant on board, and a lounge where you can dream of cruising down the river. ⓝ *Map C1 • XIII, Szent István Park, Alsó rakpart • 288 81 00 • www.fortunahajo.hu • FFF*

2 Anna

A charming hotel in the city centre. Rooms are small, but have all the amenities, while the two apartments come with classic wooden furniture and antique tables and chairs. A buffet breakfast is included. ⓝ *Map D4 • VIII, Gyulai Pál utca 14 • 327 20 00 • Dis.access • No air conditioning • www.annahotel.hu • FFF*

3 Papillon

The lovely garden, complete with a paddling pool, makes this a great choice for families. Situated in the Buda Hills, it is a good place for anyone looking for peace and quiet. There are 16 rooms – some take an extra bed. ⓝ *Map N2 • II, Rózsahegy utca 3/B • 212 47 50 • No air conditioning • www.hotels.hu/papillon • FFFFF*

4 Kulturinnov

The Kulturinnov offers basic rooms, close to Mátyás Church. The building dates from the early 20th century, and is a mix of Neo-Baroque and Neo-Gothic, blending in well with the Castle Hill surroundings. ⓝ *Map G2 • I, Szentháromság tér 6 • 355 01 22 • No air conditioning • www.mka.hu • FFFF*

5 Sissi

Named after Elizabeth (Erzsébet) – wife of Emperor Franz József II – who was known to friends as Sissi, this hotel is worthy of her name. It is a charming place with smart interiors and 44 large rooms, some with balconies. Several rooms are set aside as non-smoking. ⓝ *Map P2 • IX, Angyal utca 33 • 215 00 82 • Dis. access • No air conditioning • www.hotelsissi.hu • FFFF*

6 Astra

A charming 18th-century hotel comprising nine rooms, two suites and a family room, all housed in a historic building at the foot of the Royal Palace. Most rooms are furnished with superb antique furniture, and are set around an inner courtyard. A good breakfast is served in the arched dining room. ⓝ *Map H1 • I, Vám utca 6 • 214 19 06 • www.hotelastra.hu • FFF*

7 Mediterran

There are 40 rooms in this elegant four-star hotel, almost all of which have superb views of the Buda Hills. All the rooms are large and air conditioned. The hotel also offers secure parking. ⓝ *Map A5 • XI, Budaörsi út 20/a • 372 70 20 • Dis. access • www.hotelmediterran.hu • FFF*

8 Gizella Panzió

With its semi-Transylvanian gate, the Gizella could be in the Carpathians rather than at the foot of the Buda Hills. It is a homely place where you will be well looked after. Rooms are lovely, though not all that big. ⓝ *Map N2 • XII, Arató utca 42/b • 249 02 01 • No air conditioning • FFF*

9 Leo Panzió

In the heart of the city, the Leo Panzió (pension) is a great place for those who want to be in the thick of the action. It's a classy place, where the service is always exemplary. When it comes to value for money in downtown Budapest, this place is difficult to beat. ⓝ *Map L4 • V, Kossuth Lajos utca 2/a • 266 90 41 • FFFF*

10 Helios Hotel and Pension

A fair distance from the city centre, this is a good choice for a relaxed stay. Almost all the rooms have balconies overlooking the city. In summer, an excellent breakfast is served on the garden terrace. ⓝ *Map N2 • XII, Lidérc utca 5/a • 246 46 58 • No air conditioning • www.heliospanzio.hu • FFF*

Small hotels and pensions often charge extra for rooms with private bathrooms.

Left **Interior of the Adina Apartment Hotel** Right **The stylish Residence Izabella on Andrássy út**

Top 10 Short-Term Apartment Rentals

1 Adina Apartment Hotel

The best short-term apartments in Budapest, where no luxury has been ignored. There's a swimming pool, underground parking and 24-hour security. Prices are high but deservedly so. Long-term rents are also available. *Map C2 • XIII, Hegedűs Gyula utca 52–54 • 236 88 88 • Dis. access • www.adina.eu.com • FFFFF*

2 Apartment Hotel Victor

These are well furnished apartments near Nyugati Station. The complex has a separate entrance with a reception desk. You can have breakfast brought to your room, though all apartments are equipped with kitchens. *Map C2 • XIII, Victor Hugó utca 25–27 • 239 79 28 • www.victor.hu • FFF*

3 Central Capital Apartments

A good selection of apartments located in the central districts of Pest. Ideal for tourist, business or study trips, all have equipped kitchens and some have balconies. *Map L3 • VI, Paulay Ede utca 8 • 266 58 21 • www.rentbudapestapartment.com • FFFF*

4 Peter's Apartments

Although these are housed in an ordinary apartment block, they have tastefully decorated interiors. Located just north of Nyugati Station, they are ideally placed for the city centre. *Map C2 • XIII, Victor Hugó utca 25–27 • (30) 520 04 00 • www.peters.hu • FFF*

5 Radio Inn

These are good value one- and two-bedroom apartments near Heroes' Square, in the heart of the diplomatic district. By no means luxurious, they are well-sized, with good bathrooms. An optional breakfast is also available. *Map E3 • VI, Benczúr utca 19 • 342 83 47 • www.radioinn.hu • FF*

6 Hunguest Aparthotel Europa

Exclusive apartment hotel in the Buda Hills. Rooms range from large multi-roomed apartments to simple studios. All have kitchens and great views. A buffet breakfast is included in the price. *Map N1 • II, Hárshegyi út 5–7 • 391 23 00 • www.hunguesthotels.hu • FFFFF*

7 Residence Izabella

An apartment hotel with spacious one-, two- and three-bedroom apartments in a great location, just off Budapest's most exclusive street, Andrássy út. There is a 24-hour reception desk, security, parking and a health club. *Map D3 • VI, Izabella utca 61 • 475 59 00 • Dis. access • www.residenceizabella.com • FFFFF*

8 IBUSZ Apartments and Private Rooms

IBUSZ can arrange stays in apartments belonging to Hungarians, who are an extremely hospitable people. A great option, especially if you want to stay in central Budapest. IBUSZ also have their own apartments, available for about Ft8,000–20,000 per night. *Map L4 • V, Ferenciek tere 10 • 501 49 10 • No air conditioning • www.ibusz.hu • FF–FFF*

9 Maria and István

Three simple apartments close to the city centre, run by a friendly couple who have been taking in visitors for years. The apartments are spotlessly clean, and can house up to six people. There's a garage for your car, and if you're arriving at night, they can arrange to pick you up. *Map D6 • IX, Ferenc körút 39 • 216 07 68 • No air conditioning • No credit cards • www.mariaistvan.hu • FF*

10 To-Ma

A short-term rental agency that can either arrange lodging in apartments with Hungarian families, or in their own apartments, located all over Budapest. All apartments conform to To-Ma's standards, which are high. *Map K2 • V, Október 6 utca 22 • 353 08 19 • No air conditioning • No credit cards • FFF*

Unless otherwise stated, all apartments accept credit cards, and have private bathrooms and air conditioning.

Relaxing at the popular Back Pack Guesthouse

Price Categories

For a standard double room per night (with breakfast if included), taxes and extra charges.

F	under Ft7,500
FF	Ft7,500–15,000
FFF	Ft15,000–22,500
FFFF	Ft22,500–30,000
FFFFF	over Ft30,000

Top 10 Cheap Sleeps

1 Marco Polo Hostel

Excellent value backpacker hostel in the heart of the city, where dorms are partitioned into two-bed cubicles for privacy. Besides the dorms, there are doubles, triples and quads, all of which have en-suite facilities. There's also a bar, an Internet café, breakfast is included and there's no curfew. *Map D4 • VII, Nyár utca 6 • 413 25 55 • No air conditioning • www.marcopolohostel.com • FFF*

2 Red Bus Hostel

These are two well-run hostels with five-bed dorms, and single, double and triple rooms. There is a laundry service, no curfew and breakfast is included. *Map L4; V, Semmelweis utca 14; 266 01 36; F • Map E4; VI, Szövetség utca 35; 321 71 00; no air conditioning; www.redbusbudapest.hu; FF*

3 Best Hostel

This clean hostel is as cheap as they come, and you'll be sleeping on bunk beds with up to nine people in your room. There's no curfew, but drinking alcohol or smoking is not permitted. *Map D2 • VI, Podmaniczky utca 27 • 332 49 34 • No air conditioning • F*

4 Boat Hostel Fortuna

Most of this boat is part of a rather fine hotel *(see p115)*, but there are dorm rooms in the hull which market themselves as a hostel. These are cheaper, though more crowded, than the hotel rooms. *Map C1 • XIII, Szent István Park, Alsó rakpart • 288 81 00 • No air conditioning • www.fortunahajo.hu • FF*

5 Back Pack Guesthouse

Popular with young backpackers, this guesthouse is always buzzing. There's a courtyard, and while the rooms are spartan, they are impeccably clean and have fresh linen daily. *Map N2 • XI, Takács Menyhért utca 33 • 385 89 46 • No air conditioning • www.backpackbudapest.hu • F*

6 Citadella Hotel

The citadel atop Gellért Hill is home to one of Budapest's cheapest and best hotels, with a 14-room dormitory as well as double rooms. The only problem is the hike up at night after an evening out. *Map K6 • XI, Citadella sétány • 466 57 94 • No air conditioning • No credit cards • www.citadella.hu • F*

7 Fortuna Hostel

An ordinary hostel not in the city's best area, but close to a metro station which can take you to the city centre in minutes. Rooms are clean and staff are friendly. *Map P2 • IX, Gyáli út 3/b • 215 06 60 • No air conditioning • www.fortunahostel.hu • F*

8 Station Guesthouse

A rather rowdy hostel, but a great choice for those who enjoy late nights. The rooms are clean, bathrooms are exceptional, and there's a 24-hour bar. But if you're looking for peace and quiet, forget it. There's no curfew. *Map P1 • XIV, Mexikói út 36/b • 221 88 64 • No air conditioning • F*

9 Charles

If you can ensure that you don't get one of the noisy rooms facing the street, the Charles offers good rooms, which are more like mini-apartments with built-in kitchens. Well located on the Buda side of the river, it is home to the fine János restaurant *(see p73)*. *Map A5 • XI, Hegyalja út 23 • 212 91 69 • www.charleshotel.hu • FF*

10 Dominika Apartman Hotel

At the cheap end of the apartment sector, these superb apartments are housed inside a delightful guesthouse in a leafy Budapest suburb. There's a great terrace and swimming pool at the back. Located some distance from the city centre, this is where to come if you want luxury at a bargain price. *Map N2 • XII, Lidérc utca 13 • 246 00 62 • Dis. access • No air conditioning • www.dominika.matav.hu • FF*

Some hostels and guesthouses do not offer private bathrooms.

General Index

Acknowledgements

The Author
A linguist by training, Craig Turp has spent the majority of his adult life studying and writing about the languages and peoples of Central and Eastern Europe. He has written a number of guide books to the region, and is a key member of the team that publishes the *In Your Pocket* series of independent, locally produced city guides. He lives in Bucharest, Romania.

Main Photographer
Demetrio Carrasco

Additional Photography
Gábor Barka, Dorota and Mariusz Jarymowiczowie, Dave King, Eddie Lawrence, Rough Guides/ Eddie Gerald

Fact Checker Ágnes Ördög

AT DK INDIA:
Managing Editor Aruna Ghose
Art Editor Benu Joshi
Project Editor Vandana Mohindra
Editorial Assistance Gouri Banerji
Project Designers Shruti Singhi, Bonita Vaz
Senior Cartographer Uma Bhattacharya
Cartographer Suresh Kumar
Picture Researcher Taiyaba Khatoon
Indexer & Proofreader Pooja Kumari
DTP Co-ordinator Shailesh Sharma
DTP Designer Vinod Harish

AT DK LONDON:
Publisher Douglas Amrine
Publishing Manager Kate Poole
Senior Editor Christine Stroyan
Senior Art Editor Gadi Farfour
Senior Cartographic Editor Casper Morris
Senior DTP Designer Jason Little
DK Picture Library Romaine Werblow
Production Inderjit Bhullar

Editorial and Design Assistance
Rhiannon Furbear, Priya Kukadia, Hayley Maher, Lucy Mallows, Marianne Petrou

Picture Credits
t-top; tl-top left; tlc-top left centre; tc-top centre; tr-top right; cla-centre left above; ca-centre above; cra-centre right above; cl-centre left; c-centre; cr-centre right; clb-centre left below; cb-centre below; crb-centre right below; bl-bottom left; b-bottom; bc-bottom centre; bcl-bottom centre left; br-bottom right; d-detail.

Every effort has been made to trace the copyright holders of images, and we apologize in advance for any unintentional omissions. We would be pleased to insert the appropriate acknowledgements in any subsequent edition of this publication.

The publishers would also like to thank the following for their assistance and kind permission to photograph at their establishments: Academy of Sciences; Adina Apartment Hotel; Tímea Adrián, Statue Park; Ba Bar; Budapest Transport Ltd; Centrál Kávéház; Cotton House; Eva Fisli, Hungarian National Museum; Fat Mo's; Ferenc Liszt Museum; András Gabányi, Hungarian Parliament; Gerbeaud Cukrászda; Katalin Gyorfi, Budapest Festival Centre; Judit Mihalcsik and Vanda Horvath, Tourism Office of Budapest; Máté Istvánné, St Stephen's Basilica; Kempinski Hotel Corvinus Budapest; Kisbuda Gyöngye Étterem; Poloskey Krisztina, Mátyás Church; Vásony Mihály, Danubius Hotel Gellért; Emese Soós, State Opera House; St Anne's Church; WestEnd City

Center; and all other churches, museums, parks, hotels, restaurants and sights too numerous to thank individually.

The publishers would like to thank the following individuals, companies and picture libraries for their kind permission to reproduce their photographs. ALAMY: E.J. Baumeister Jr. 7crb, 109tr; Chris Fredriksson 17c,100–101; f1 online 27cr; Sergio Pitamitz 84br. ARANYSZARVAS RESTAURANT 73tl.

ALFRED MOLON: 24–5c. THE BRIDGEMAN ART LIBRARY: The Visitation, 1506 Master M.S., (16th century) Magyar Nemzeti Galeria, Budapest 20bc; Picnic in May, Szinyei-Merse, Pál (1845–1920) Magyar Nemzeti Galeria, Budapest 21tc; Birdsong Ferenczy, Károly (1862–1917) Magyar Nemzeti Galeria, Budapest 21cra; Woman Bathing, Lotz, Károly (1833–1907) Magyar Nemzeti Galeria, Budapest 21bc; The Golden Age, detail (Oil on Canvas), Vaszary, János (1867–1939) Magyar Nemzeti Galeria, Budapest 22tl; Girl with a Bird Cage, Rippl-Rónai, József (1861–1927) Magyar Nemzeti Galeria, Budapest 22bl; Birth of Mary, Brixen, Leinhart von (fl.1453–74) Museum of Fine Arts, Budapest 38bl; BUDAPEST FESTIVAL CENTRE: 48tl, 48ca.

CORBIS: 4–5; Austrian Archives 34c; Dallas and John Heaton 6crb, 16–17c; Hulton-Deutsch Collection 35br; Catherine Karnow 19cr, 26–7c; Yevgeny Khaldei 34tc; Craig Lovell 38tc; SYGMA/Bernard Bisson 34tr; Adam Woolfitt 38tl.

EKLEKTIKA CAFE: 55tl.

GERBEAUD GASZTRONOMIA Kft.: 3tr, 52tr. HUNGARIAN NATIONAL MUSEUM: 31tr; András Dabasi 31ca, 31bc; Bence Képessy 30br, 38tr; Károly Szelényi 30cb.

LONELY PLANET IMAGES: Kim Grant 48br; Martin Moos 11br, 39tl.

MARY EVANS PICTURE LIBRARY: 34tl. MASTERFILE: Russell Monk 46–7. PHOTOLIBRARY: 28–9; 80–81.

RED DOT, BUDAPEST: Tamas Reichel 92tl; RESTAURANT GUNDEL: 53tl; REUTERS: Balazs Gardi 35bl; STR 49tl. ROBERT HARDING WORLD IMAGERY: Digital Vision 1c. VIPARTS: Gábor Szilágyi 48tr.

All other images are © Dorling Kindersley. For further information see www.dkimages.com

Phrase Book

In an Emergency

Help!	**Segítség!**	**sheg**eetshayg!
Stop!	**Stop!**	shtop!
Call a doctor	**Hívjon orvost!**	**heev**yon **or**vosht!
Call an ambulance	**Hívjon mentőt!**	heevyon menturt
Call the police	**Hívja a rendőrséget**	**heev**ya a **ren**-dur **shay**get
Call the fire department	**Hívja a tűzoltókat!**	**heev**ya a **tewz**oltowkot!
Where is the nearest telephone?	**Hol van a legközelebbi telefon?**	hol von uh **leg**kurze-lebbi **tel**efon?
Where is the nearest hospital?	**Hol van a legközelebbi kórház?**	hol von a **leg**-kurze-lebbi **koor**hahz?

Communications Essentials

Yes/No	**Igen/Nem**	**ig**en/nem
Please (offering)	**Tessék**	**tesh**ayk
Please (asking)	**Kérem**	**kay**rem
Thank you	**Köszönöm**	**kurss**urnurm
No, thank you	**Köszönöm nem**	**kurss**urnurm nem
Excuse me, please	**Bocsánatot kérek**	**boch**anutot **kay**rek
Hello	**Jó napot**	yow **nop**ot
Goodbye	**Viszontlátásra**	**viss**ont-latashruh
What?	**Mi?**	mi?
When?	**Mikor?**	**mi**kor?
Why?	**Miért?**	**mi**ayrt?
Where?	**Hol?**	hol?

Useful Phrases

How are you?	**Hogy van?**	**hod**-yuh vun?
Very well, thank you	**köszönöm nagyon jól**	**kurss**urnurm **noj**jon yowl
Pleased to meet you	**Örülök hogy megismerhettem**	**ur**-rewlurk **hod**-yuh **meg**ish-merhettem
Where can I get…?	**Hol kaphatok …-t?**	hol **kup**hutok …-t?
How do you get to?	**Hogy lehet …-ba eljutni?**	**hod**-yuh **leh**et …-buh **el**-yootni?
Do you speak English?	**Beszél angolul?**	**bess**ayl **ung**olool?
I can't speak Hungarian	**Nem beszélek magyarul**	nem **bess**aylek **mud**-yarool
I don't understand	**Nem értem**	nem **ayr**tem
Can you help me?	**Kérhetem a segítségét?**	**kayr**hetem uh **sheg**-eechaygayt
Please speak slowly	**Tessék lassabban beszélni**	**tesh**ayk **lush**ubbun **bess**aylni
Sorry!	**Elnézést!**	**el**nayzaysht!

Useful Words

big	**nagy**	noj
small	**kicsi**	**kich**i
hot	**forró**	**for**ow
cold	**hideg**	**hid**eg
good	**jó**	yow
bad	**rossz**	ross
open	**nyitva**	**nyit**va
closed	**zárva**	**zar**va
left	**bal**	bol
right	**jobb**	yob
entrance	**bejárat**	**beh**-yarut
exit	**kijárat**	**ki**-yarut
toilet	**WC**	vaytsay
free/unoccupied	**szabad**	**sobb**od
free/no charge	**ingyen**	**in**jen

Making a Telephone Call

Can I call abroad from here?	**Telefonálhatok innen külföldre?**	**tel**efonalhutok **in**en **kewl**furldreh?
Could I leave a message?	**Hagyhatnék egy üzenetet?**	**hud**-yuhutnayk ed-yuh **ewz**enetet?
Hold on	**Várjon!**	**vahr**-yon!

Shopping

How much is this?	**Ez mennyibe kerül?**	ez **menn**-yibeh **ke**rewl?
Do you have…?	**Kapható önöknél…?**	**kup**hutaw **urn**urknayl?
Do you take credit cards?	**Elfogadják a hitelkártyákat?**	**el**fogud-yak uh **hi**telkart-yakut?
What time do you open/close?	**Hánykor nyitnak/zárnak?**	**Hahn** kor nyitnak/zarnak?
this one	**ez**	ez
expensive	**drága**	**drah**ga
cheap	**olcsó**	**ol**chow
size	**méret**	**may**ret
white	**fehér**	**fe**heer
black	**fekete**	**fe**keteh
red	**piros**	**pi**rosh
yellow	**sárga**	**shar**ga
green	**zöld**	zurld
blue	**kék**	cake
brown	**barna**	**bor**na

Types of Shop

antiques dealer	**antikvárius**	**on**tikvahrioosh
bank	**bank**	bonk
bookshop	**könyvesbolt**	**kurn**-yuveshbolt
cake shop	**cukrászda**	**tsook**rassduh
chemist	**patika**	**pu**tikuh
department store	**áruház**	**ar**oo-haz
florist	**virágüzlet**	**vi**rag-ewzlet
market	**piac**	**pi**-uts
newsagent	**újságos**	**oo**-yushagosh
post office	**postahivatal**	**posh**ta-hivatal
shoe shop	**cipőbolt**	**tsi**purbolt
souvenir shop	**ajándékbolt**	**uy**-yandaykbolt
supermarket	**élelmiszerbolt**	**a**baytsay
tobacconist	**trafikos**	**tra**fikos
travel agent	**utazási iroda**	**oot**uzashi iroduh

Staying in a Hotel

Have you any vacancies?	**Van kiadó szobájuk?**	vun **ki**-udaw soba-yook?
double room with double bed	**francia-ágyas szoba**	**front**sia-**ah**josh **sob**uh
twin room	**kétágyas szoba**	**kaytad**-yush **sob**uh
single room	**egyágyas szoba**	**ed-yad**-yush **sob**uh
room with a bath/shower	**fürdőszobás/ zuhanyzós szoba**	**fewr**dur-**sob**ahsh/**zoo**-honzahsh soba
porter	**portás**	**por**tahsh
key	**kulcs**	koolch
I have a reservation	**Foglaltam egy szobát**	**fog**lultum ed-yuh **sob**at

Sightseeing

bus	**autóbusz**	**ow**tawbooss
tram	**villamos**	**vil**lumosh
train	**vonat**	**von**ut
underground	**metró**	**met**raw
bus stop	**buszmegálló**	**booss megallaw**
art gallery	**képcsarnok**	**kayp**-chornok
palace	**palota**	**pol**ola
church	**templom**	**temp**lom
garden	**kert**	kert
library	**könyvtár**	**kurn**vtar
museum	**múzeum**	**moo**zayoom
tourist information	**túristahivatal**	**toor**ishta-hivotol
closed for public holiday	**ünnepnap zárva**	**ewn**-nepnap **zar**va

Eating Out

A table for… please	**Egy asztalt szeretnék… személyre**	ed-yuh **uss**tult **ser**etnayk… **sem**ayreh
I want to reserve a table	**Szeretnékegy asztalt foglalni**	**ser**etnayk **ed**-yuh **uss**tult **fog**lolni
The bill please	**Kérem a szamlát**	**kay**rem uh **sam**lat
I am a vegetarian	**Vegetáriánnus vagyok**	**veg**etari-ahnoosh **voj**ok
I'd like…	**Szeretnék egy…-t**	**ser**et nayk ed-yuh…-t
waiter/waitress	**pincér/pincérnő**	**pints**ayr/ **pints**ayrnur
menu	**étlap**	**ayt**lup
wine list	**itallap**	**it**ullup
glass	**pohár**	pohar
bottle	**üveg**	**ew**veg
knife	**kés**	kaysh
fork	**villa**	villuh
spoon	**kanál**	**kun**al
breakfast	**reggeli**	**reg**-geli
lunch	**ebéd**	**eb**ayd
dinner	**vacsora**	**voch**ora
main courses	**főételek**	**fur**-aytelek
starters	**előételek**	**el**ur-aytelek
desserts	**édességek**	**ayd**esh-shaydek
rare	**angolosan**	**ongo**loshan
well done	**átsütve**	**aht**shewtveh

Menu Decoder

ásványvíz	**ahsh**vahnveez	mineral water
bárány	**bah**rahn	lamb
bors	borsh	pepper
csirke	**cheer**keh	chicken
csokoládé	**chok**olahday	chocolate
cukor	**tsook**or	sugar
ecet	**ets**et	vinegar
fagylalt	**fod**yuhloot	ice cream
fehérbor	**fe**heerbor	white wine
fokhagyma	**fok**hodyuhma	garlic
főtt	furt	boiled
gomba	**gom**ba	mushrooms
gyümölcs	**dyew**murlch	fruit
gyümölcslé	**dyew**murlch-lay	fruit juice
hagyma	**hoj**ma	onions
hal	hol	fish
hús	hoosh	meat
kávé	**ka**vay	coffee
kenyér	**ken**-yeer	bread
krumpli	**kroom**pli	potatoes
kolbász	**kol**bahss	sausage
leves	levesh	soup
marha	**mar**ha	beef
mustár	**moosh**tahr	mustard
paradicsom	**por**odichom	tomatoes
párolt	**pah**rolt	steamed
rizs	rizh	rice
bifsztek	**bif**stek	steak
roston	**rosh**ton	grilled
sajt	shoyt	cheese
saláta	**shol**ahta	salad
sertéshús	**sher**taysh-hoosh	pork
só	shaw	salt
sonka	**shon**ka	ham
sör	shur	beer
sült	shewlt	fried/roasted
sült burgonya	shewlt **boor**gonya	chips
sütemény	**shew**temayn-yuh	cake, pastry
tea	**tay**-uh	tea
tej	tay	milk
tejszín	**tay**sseen	cream
tengeri hal	**teng**eri hol	seafood
tojás	**toy**ahsh	egg
vörösbor	**vur**-rurshbor	red wine
zsemle	**zhem**leh	roll
zsemlegombóc	**zhem**leh-**gom**bowts	dumplings

Numbers

0	**nulla**	**nool**luh
1	**egy**	**ed**-yuh
2	**kettő, két**	**ket**tur, kayt
3	**három**	**har**om
4	**négy**	**nayd**-yuh
5	**öt**	urt
6	**hat**	hut
7	**hét**	hayt
8	**nyolc**	**n**-yolts
9	**kilenc**	**ki**lents
10	**tíz**	teez
11	**tizenegy**	**tiz**ened-yuh
12	**tizenkettő**	**tiz**enkettur
13	**tizenhárom**	**tiz**enharom
14	**tizennégy**	**tiz**en-nayd-yuh
15	**tizenöt**	**tiz**enurt
16	**tizenhat**	**tiz**enhut
17	**tizenhét**	**tiz**enhayt
18	**tizennyolc**	**tiz**enn-yolts
19	**tizenkilenc**	**tiz**enkilents
20	**húsz**	hooss
30	**harminc**	**hur**mints
40	**negyven**	**ned**-yuven
50	**ötven**	**urt**ven
60	**hatvan**	**hut**vun
70	**hetven**	**het**ven
80	**nyolcvan**	**n-yolts**vun
90	**kilencven**	**ki**lentsven
100	**száz**	saz
1,000	**ezer**	**ez**er
10,000	**tízezer**	**teez**ezer
1,000,000	**millió**	**mil**liaw

Time

one minute	**egy perc**	**ed**-yuh perts
hour	**óra**	**aw**ruh
half an hour	**félóra**	**fayla**wruh
Sunday	**vasárnap**	**vush**arnup
Monday	**hétfő**	**hayt**fur
Tuesday	**kedd**	kedd
Wednesday	**szerda**	serduh
Thursday	**csütörtök**	**chew**turturk
Friday	**péntek**	**payn**tek
Saturday	**szombat**	**som**but

Selected Street Index